This book belongs to

....

Date

....

An All-in-One Study
on the Life of Jesus

the gospels

An All-in-One Study on the Life of Jesus

the gospels

THE
BIBLE STUDY
COLLECTIVE

BARBOUR
PUBLISHING

Editorial assistance by Tracy M. Sumner and Carey Scott.

ISBN 979-8-89151-033-3

Cover Design: Greg Jackson, Thinkpen Design

Published by Barbour Publishing, Inc., 1810 Barbour Drive, Uhrichsville, Ohio 44683, www.barbourbooks.com

Our mission is to inspire the world with the life-changing message of the Bible.

Printed in China.

Contents

THE BIBLE STUDY COLLECTIVE

Welcome to *The Gospels: An All-in-One Study on the Life of Jesus*, a collection of thirty select passages from the four Gospels (Matthew, Mark, Luke, and John) as well as guidance and encouragement for digging into them yourself.

The Gospels are written accounts of the life of Jesus Christ—each recorded from a different perspective. They include details of Jesus' birth, His childhood, His earthly ministry (His teaching and miracles), and His death and resurrection. Two of the Gospels, Matthew and John, were written by apostles (the original disciples Jesus called to follow Him), while Mark and Luke were written by men outside that group.

Each study in this guide includes an introduction of the particular Gospel passage on the first page, followed by the full text of the passage on the next. The third through the fifth pages of each study highlight the three steps of what is called the "inductive method" of Bible study: observation, interpretation, and application. Here's how it works:

- *Observation* answers the question "What does it say?" In other words, what is the actual content in the text?
- *Interpretation* answers the question "What does it mean?" In this step, you'll consider the author's original intent and meaning.
- Finally, *application* answers the questions "What does it mean to you—and how can you apply it to your life?"

Each study in this guide ends with a select verse (or verses) from the Gospel passage you've just studied, as well as related scriptures for memorization and meditation.

Our prayer is that *The Gospels: An All-in-One Study on the Life of Jesus* will help you to better understand God's Word and to apply its timeless truth to your own life of faith in the Lord Jesus Christ.

Barbour Publishing

Study 1

MATTHEW 5:1–16

Jesus' ministry on earth included much memorable preaching and teaching. The highlight may be His famous "Sermon on the Mount" (Matthew 5–7). In this remarkable sermon, Jesus delivered practical and difficult teaching that helped to reshape His followers' understanding of the law of Moses.

Jesus opened His sermon by speaking what we call the "Beatitudes," or statements of blessing. Each of these statements begins with the words "blessed are. . ." and then goes on to say who is blessed and why.

Throughout scripture God calls His people to live by standards very different than those of the world. We are not just to behave differently but to be different in our attitudes and thinking. That is one of the overarching themes of the Sermon on the Mount, and specifically the Beatitudes.

Matthew 5:1–16 Study Outline

(VERSES 1–2)	Jesus begins teaching
(VERSES 3–10)	The people God blesses, and why
(VERSES 11–12)	The blessings of being persecuted, and of loving God and His Word
(VERSES 13–16)	Being salt and light

The Beatitudes

1And seeing the multitudes, He went up on a mountain, and
when He was seated, His disciples came to Him. 2And He
opened His mouth and taught them, saying,

> 3"Blessed are the poor in spirit, for theirs is the kingdom of heaven.
> 4Blessed are those who mourn, for they shall be comforted.
> 5Blessed are the meek, for they shall inherit the earth.
> 6Blessed are those who hunger and thirst after righteousness, for they shall be filled.
> 7Blessed are the merciful, for they shall obtain mercy.
> 8Blessed are the pure in heart, for they shall see God.
> 9Blessed are the peacemakers, for they shall be called the children of God.
> 10Blessed are those who are persecuted for righteousness' sake, for theirs is the kingdom of heaven.

11"Blessed are you when men revile you and persecute
you, and say all manner of evil against you falsely for My
sake. 12Rejoice and be exceedingly glad, for great is your
reward in heaven, for so they persecuted the prophets who
were before you.

13"You are the salt of the earth, but if the salt has lost its savor, with what shall it be salted? It is thereafter good for nothing but to be cast out and to be trampled underfoot by men.

14"You are the light of the world. A city that is set on a
hill cannot be hidden. 15Nor do men light a candle and put it
under a bushel, but on a candlestick, and it gives light to all
who are in the house. 16Let your light so shine before men,
that they may see your good works and glorify your Father
who is in heaven."

Observe

What do the Beatitudes say about what it takes to live a blessed life?

What do verses 11–12 say about understanding and responding to opposition and persecution?

What did Jesus say about being salt and light?

Interpret

What did Jesus mean when He used the word *blessed*?

What does it mean to be poor in spirit, and what does it have to do with inheriting the kingdom of heaven?

What does it mean to be salt and light in this world?

Apply

How can you be a more merciful person—and why does that matter?

What needs to change so you can be a peacemaker in every area of your life?

How and why should you focus each day on being light in this world?

Matthew 5:1–16 Scripture for Memorization/Meditation

"Let your light so shine before men,
that they may see your good works and
glorify your Father who is in heaven."
VERSE 16

Verses for Further Memorization/Meditation

- And all things are from God, who has reconciled us to Himself through Jesus Christ and has given to us the ministry of reconciliation—namely, that God was in Christ reconciling the world to Himself, not imputing their trespasses to them, and has committed to us the word of reconciliation (2 Corinthians 5:18–19).
- For to you it is given on behalf of Christ, not only to believe in Him, but also to suffer for His sake (Philippians 1:29).
- And whatever you do in word or deed, do all in the name of the Lord Jesus, giving thanks to God the Father by Him (Colossians 3:17).

Study 2

LUKE 5:1–11

Jesus was about to begin His earthly ministry, and it was now time for Him to gather together twelve disciples, the men who would travel with, observe, and learn from Him for the next three years . . .then take His message of salvation to the world around them.

Luke 5:1–11 tells of Jesus teaching crowds at the Lake of Gennesaret. Afterward, He invited three fishermen—Peter, James, and John—to follow Him and "catch men." Jesus performed a shocking miracle that showed these disciples not just who He was but who He would be to them from that day forward.

As you read this passage, pay special attention to the new disciples' reactions to what they have just seen.

Luke 5:1–11 Study Outline

(VERSES 1–3)	Jesus teaches from a fishing boat
(VERSE 4)	Jesus' instruction and the fishermen's response
(VERSES 5–7)	The miraculous catch of fish
(VERSE 8)	Simon Peter's response to a miracle
(VERSES 9–11)	Jesus' call to discipleship

Calling the First Disciples

1 And it came to pass, that as the people pressed on Him to
hear the word of God, He stood by the lake of Gennesaret
2 and saw two ships standing by the lake. But the fishermen
had gone out of them and were washing their nets. 3 And He
entered into one of the ships, which was Simon's, and asked
him to thrust out a little from the land. And He sat down and
taught the people out of the ship.

4 Now when He had finished speaking, He said to Simon,
"Launch out into the deep and let down your nets for a catch."

5 And Simon answered and said to Him, "Master, we have
toiled all the night and have taken nothing. Nevertheless, at
Your word I will let down the net." 6 And when they had done
this, they caught a great multitude of fish, and their net was
breaking. 7 And they beckoned to their partners who were in
the other ship, that they should come and help them. And
they came and filled both the ships, so that they began to
sink. 8 When Simon Peter saw it, he fell down at Jesus' knees,
saying, "Depart from me, for I am a sinful man, O Lord."

9 For he and all who were with him were astonished at the
catch of the fish that they had taken. 10 And so also were James
and John, the sons of Zebedee, who were partners with Simon.
And Jesus said to Simon, "Do not fear. From now on you shall
catch men." 11 And when they had brought their ships to land,
they forsook all and followed Him.

Observe

What command did Jesus give Simon?

How did Simon respond to the miraculous catch of fish?

What specific words did Jesus use to call Simon to ministry?

Interpret

Why did Jesus choose to minister from Simon's fishing boat?

Why would Simon push Jesus away after witnessing such a wonderful miracle? Why did he not simply fall on his face and worship the Lord?

How did this miracle help to shape the way these fishermen viewed Jesus?

In the past, how have you responded to Jesus interrupting your schedule or plans? How will you respond moving forward?

When has Jesus shown you He is far greater than your best abilities? How did that revelation build or strengthen your faith?

What would it look like to forsake all and follow Jesus? How can you realistically walk that out daily?

Luke 5:1–11 Scripture for Memorization/Meditation

Jesus said to Simon, "Do not fear. From now on you shall catch men." And when they had brought their ships to land, they forsook all and followed Him.
verses 10–11

Verses for Further Memorization/Meditation

- And Samuel said, "Has the Lord as great delight in burnt offerings and sacrifices as in obeying the voice of the Lord? Behold, to obey is better than sacrifice and to listen than the fat of rams" (1 Samuel 15:22).
- "Certainly I will be with you. And this shall be a sign to you that I have sent you: when you have brought forth the people out of Egypt, you shall serve God on this mountain" (Exodus 3:12).
- But the fruit of the Spirit is love, joy, peace, long-suffering, gentleness, goodness, faith, meekness, self-control. Against such there is no law (Galatians 5:22–23).
- But the Lord said to him, "Go your way, for he is a chosen vessel for Me, to bear My name before the Gentiles and kings and the children of Israel. For I will show him how much he must suffer for My name's sake" (Acts 9:15–16).

Study 3

JOHN 2:1–11

The four Gospels record some three dozen miracles performed by Jesus, the first His turning water into wine at a wedding in Cana of Galilee. Jesus saved face for the wedding host, for it was a major social faux pas to run out of wine at such a celebration.

At His mother Mary's request, Jesus transformed about 120 gallons of water into high-quality wine. Jesus saved the day for the wedding host and began a ministry that included even more spectacular acts that brought glory to His Father in heaven. His miracles also provided evidence that Jesus was worthy of men and women's faith.

In bringing the problem to Jesus and then instructing the wedding servants to do as Jesus said, Mary showed that she was a woman of faith.

John 2:1 11 Study Outline

(VERSES 1–2)	Jesus and His disciples are invited to the wedding in Cana
(VERSES 3–4)	Mary brings a problem to Jesus, and He responds
(VERSE 5)	Mary acts in faith
(VERSES 6–8)	The miracle of changing water into wine
(VERSES 9–10)	The high quality of the wine
(VERSE 11)	The disciples' response

The Wedding at Cana: The First Miracle

1 And the third day there was a wedding in Cana of Galilee,
and the mother of Jesus was there. 2 And both Jesus and His
disciples were called to the wedding. 3 And when they lacked
wine, the mother of Jesus said to Him, “They have no wine.”

4 Jesus said to her, “Woman, what have I to do with you?
My hour has not yet come.”

5 His mother said to the servants, “Whatever He says to
you, do it.”

6 And there were set there six waterpots of stone, according
to the manner of the purifying of the Jews, containing two or
three firkins apiece. 7 Jesus said to them, “Fill the waterpots
with water.” And they filled them up to the brim. 8 And He said
to them, “Draw some out now, and take it to the master of the
feast.” And they took it.

9 When the master of the feast had tasted the water that
was made wine and did not know where it was from (but the
servants who drew the water knew), the master of the feast
called the bridegroom 10 and said to him, “Every man at the
beginning sets out good wine, and when men have well drunk,
then what is worse. But you have kept the good wine until now.”

11 This beginning of miracles Jesus did in Cana of Galilee
and revealed His glory. And His disciples believed in Him.

Observe

Why were Jesus and His disciples at the wedding in Cana?

What problem did His mother ask Jesus to solve at the wedding? What was His reaction?

How did Mary respond when Jesus seemed reluctant to help her? What was the outcome?

Interpret

What does Mary's behavior toward the wedding host, who was running out of wine, indicate about her?

What does Jesus' answer to Mary reveal about Him and His relationship with her?

How did the disciples react to what they had seen Jesus do? How did it help shape their faith in Him?

Apply

What do you normally do when faced with a problem or difficulty? How do Mary's faith-filled responses affect you?

When waiting on God to bring the help you have prayerfully requested of Him, how can you stay hopeful and expectant?

In what ways do you acknowledge God's goodness when He's showed up for you in mighty ways?

John 2:1–11 Scripture for Memorization/Meditation

His mother said to the servants,
"Whatever He says to you, do it."
VERSE 5

This beginning of miracles Jesus did in Cana of Galilee and revealed His glory. And His disciples believed in Him.
VERSE 11

Verses for Further Memorization/Meditation

- "And all things, whatever you ask in prayer, believing, you shall receive" (Matthew 21:22).
- Therefore let us come boldly to the throne of grace, that we may obtain mercy and find grace to help in time of need (Hebrews 4:16).
- But without faith it is impossible to please Him, for he who comes to God must believe that He is, and that He is a rewarder of those who diligently seek Him (Hebrews 11:6).

Study 4

LUKE 7:36–49

In Luke 7:36–49, Jesus has been invited to a dinner at the home of a Pharisee named Simon. He showed those in attendance that He had come to forgive and save not just those of high social standing but even the worst of sinners.

As Jesus and the rest of the guests sat down to eat, a particularly notorious sinner—an unnamed woman who was very likely a prostitute—began washing Jesus' feet with her tears, drying them with her hair, and kissing and anointing them with ointment.

Clearly, this woman knew who she was—but more importantly, she showed that she knew who Jesus was and what He could do for her. For that reason, she courageously entered the home of a powerful Jewish religious leader and revealed her love for Jesus.

Luke 7:36–49 Study Outline

(VERSE 36)	A Jewish religious leader named Simon hosts Jesus for a meal
(VERSES 37–38)	A sinful woman arrives at Simon's home and honors Jesus
(VERSE 39)	Simon is shocked that Jesus would allow such a woman to touch Him
(VERSES 40–47)	Jesus teaches Simon on the nature of forgiveness
(VERSES 48–49)	Jesus openly forgives the woman for her sins, astonishing those in attendance

A Parable and an Example of Forgiveness

36 And one of the Pharisees asked Him to eat with him. And
He went into the Pharisee's house and sat down at the table.
37 And, behold, a woman in the city who was a sinner, when
she knew that Jesus sat at the table in the Pharisee's house,
brought an alabaster box of ointment, 38 and stood at His feet
behind Him weeping, and began to wash His feet with tears, and
wiped them with the hair of her head, and kissed His feet, and
anointed them with the ointment. 39 Now when the Pharisee who
had invited Him saw it, he spoke to himself, saying, "If He were
a prophet, this Man would have known who and what manner
of woman this is who is touching Him, for she is a sinner."

40 And Jesus answered and said to him, "Simon, I have something to say to you." And he said, "Master, say it."

41 "There was a certain creditor who had two debtors. The
one owed five hundred pence, and the other fifty. 42 And when
they had nothing to pay, he freely forgave them both. Tell Me,
therefore, which of them will love him most?"

43 Simon answered and said, "I suppose he to whom he forgave most."

And He said to him, "You have judged rightly." 44 And He
turned to the woman and said to Simon, "Do you see this woman?
I entered into your house. You gave Me no water for My feet,
but she has washed My feet with tears and wiped them with
the hair of her head. 45 You gave me no kiss, but this woman has
not ceased to kiss My feet since the time I came in. 46 You did
not anoint My head with oil, but this woman has anointed My
feet with ointment. 47 Therefore I say to you, her sins, which are
many, are forgiven, for she loved much. But to whom little is
forgiven, the same loves little."

48 And He said to her, "Your sins are forgiven."

49 And those who sat at the table with Him began to say to themselves, "Who is this who also forgives sins?"

Observe

What did the sinful woman do once she was in Jesus' presence?

What did Simon the Pharisee think of Jesus allowing such a notoriously sinful woman to touch Him?

Jesus knew what Simon was thinking. How did He respond?

Interpret

How did Jesus know what Simon was thinking? Why would He choose to teach Simon and not strongly rebuke him?

Why did the sinful woman show Jesus such affection and reverence?

What does this passage show you about God's forgiveness through Jesus?

Apply

How does Jesus' short parable of the moneylenders encourage you? What does it demonstrate about the nature of God's willingness to forgive your sins?

What kind of attitude does this passage encourage you to have toward those who have lived a life of sin?

In what ways can you show Jesus honor and gratitude with the same spirit of humility as the sinful woman?

Luke 7:36–49 Scripture for Memorization/Meditation

He said to her, "Your sins are forgiven." And those who sat at the table with Him began to say to themselves, "Who is this who also forgives sins?"
VERSES 48–49

Verses for Further Memorization/Meditation

- Therefore if any man is in Christ, he is a new creature. Old things have passed away; behold, all things have become new (2 Corinthians 5:17).
- [God] has delivered us from the power of darkness and has translated us to the kingdom of His dear Son, in whom we have redemption through His blood, even the forgiveness of sins (Colossians 1:13–14).
- Who is a God like You, who pardons guilt and passes by the transgression of the remnant of His heritage? He does not retain His anger forever, because He delights in mercy (Micah 7:18).
- My little children, I write these things to you, that you may not sin. And if any man sins, we have an advocate with the Father, Jesus Christ the righteous. And He is the propitiation for our sins, and not for ours only, but also for the sins of the whole world (1 John 2:1–2).

Study 5

JOHN 8:1–11

In one of the best-known Gospel accounts of Jesus' encounters with sinners who needed Him, Jewish religious leaders brought Him an adulterous woman—one caught in the very act—and asked if she should be stoned to death as the law of Moses had commanded.

His enemies thought they had Jesus trapped: If He approved of the stoning, He would appear harsh and cruel. If He told them to let her go, they could accuse Jesus of breaking the law of Moses.

He didn't directly answer the woman's accusers. Instead, Jesus simply told them the one without sin could cast the first stone. They soon turned away, leaving Jesus alone with the woman. Then He allowed her to go her way with the encouragement to "sin no more."

JOHN 8:1–11 STUDY OUTLINE

(VERSES 1–2)	Jesus teaching at the temple
(VERSES 3–5)	Religious leaders bring an adulterous woman to Jesus and ask if she should be stoned to death for her sin
(VERSES 6–8)	In front of the scribes and Pharisees, Jesus shows the woman compassion and mercy
(VERSE 9)	The chastened religious leaders leave Jesus alone with the woman
(VERSES 10–11)	Jesus assures the woman that He doesn't condemn her; she should "sin no more."

Two Responses to a Woman Caught in Sin

[1]Jesus went to the Mount of Olives. [2]And early in the morning He came again into the temple, and all the people came to Him. And He sat down and taught them. [3]And the scribes and Pharisees brought to Him a woman caught in adultery. And when they had set her in the midst, [4]they said to Him, "Master, this woman was caught in adultery, in the very act. [5]Now Moses, in the Law, commanded us that such should be stoned. But what do You say?"

[6]They said this, tempting Him, that they might have reason to accuse Him. But Jesus stooped down and with His finger wrote on the ground, as though He did not hear them. [7]So when they continued asking Him, He lifted Himself up and said to them, "He who is without sin among you, let him first cast a stone at her." [8]And again He stooped down and wrote on the ground.

[9]And those who heard it, being convicted by their own consciences, went out one by one, beginning at the eldest, even to the last. And Jesus was left alone, and the woman standing in the midst. [10]When Jesus had lifted Himself up and saw none but the woman, He said to her, "Woman, where are those accusers of yours? Has no man condemned you?"

[11]She said, "No man, Lord."

And Jesus said to her, "Neither do I condemn you. Go and sin no more."

Observe

What sin had this woman committed before the Pharisees brought her to Jesus? What did the law of Moses say should be done with her?

How did Jesus respond to the woman's accusers?

What message did Jesus speak to this woman after the Pharisees had left her alone with Him?

Interpret

JOHN 8:1–11

How did the Pharisees attempt to set a trap for Jesus? What would they accuse Him of if He simply told them to let the adulterous woman go?

How does Jesus approach our sin today?

Jesus assured the adulterous woman that He didn't condemn her. But did that free her to continue in her sinful behavior, or did Jesus free her to change her life choices?

Apply

What does this passage say about condemning others for their obvious sins? Does it challenge you or bring comfort?

What does this encounter teach you about how to view your own past sins—or the past sins of your friends?

What changes do you need to make in your actions or attitudes so that your life pleases the Lord and deepens your faith?

John 8:1–11 Scripture for Memorization/Meditation

When Jesus had lifted Himself up and saw none but the woman, He said to her, "Woman, where are those accusers of yours? Has no man condemned you?" She said, "No man, Lord." And Jesus said to her, "Neither do I condemn you. Go and sin no more."
VERSES 10–11

Verses for Further Memorization/Meditation

- [Jesus], being the brightness of His glory and the express image of His person, and upholding all things by the word of His power, when He had by Himself purged our sins, sat down at the right hand of the Majesty on high (Hebrews 1:3).
- If we confess our sins, He is faithful and just to forgive us our sins and to cleanse us from all unrighteousness (1 John 1:9).
- "God did not send His Son into the world to condemn the world but that the world might be saved through Him. He who believes in Him is not condemned, but he who does not believe is condemned already because he has not believed in the name of the only begotten Son of God" (John 3:17–18).
- Submit yourselves, therefore, to God. Resist the devil and he will flee from you. Draw near to God and He will draw near to you. Cleanse your hands, you sinners, and purify your hearts, you double-minded (James 4:7–8).

Study 6

JOHN 11:20–40

John 11:1–46 tells the beautiful story of Jesus miraculously raising His friend Lazarus from the dead. Jesus knew that Lazarus was sick to the point of death, but He waited two days before traveling to Bethany, Lazarus' hometown. Jesus wasn't just waiting for His friend to die. Instead, He went to Bethany afterward so that He could glorify His Father not only by performing a great miracle but by teaching Mary and Martha, the man's sisters, a valuable lesson about faith.

As Jesus arrives, Martha runs to Him to express her disappointment and grief—and her faith. Jesus knew what He was going to do that day. But first, He would teach Martha and Mary what could happen—if only they believed.

John 11:20–40 Study Outline

(VERSES 20–22)	Martha's complaint—and her faith
(VERSES 23–26)	Jesus' resurrection promises
(VERSE 27)	Martha's words of faith
(VERSES 28–32)	Mary goes to Jesus
(VERSES 33–38)	Jesus responds to the people's grief
(VERSES 39–40)	Jesus prepares to demonstrate the glory of God

Jesus in Bethany

20Then Martha, as soon as she heard that Jesus was coming,
went and met Him, but Mary still sat in the house. 21Then
Martha said to Jesus, "Lord, if You had been here, my brother
would not have died. 22But even now I know that whatever
You will ask of God, God will give it You."

23Jesus said to her, "Your brother shall rise again."

24Martha said to Him, "I know that he shall rise again in
the resurrection on the last day."

25Jesus said to her, "I am the resurrection and the life. He
who believes in Me, though he were dead, yet shall he live.
26And whoever lives and believes in Me shall never die. Do
you believe this?"

27She said to Him, "Yes, Lord, I believe that You are the
Christ, the Son of God, who is coming into the world." 28And
when she had said this, she went her way and called Mary
her sister secretly, saying, "The Master has come and calls
for you." 29As soon as she heard that, she arose quickly and
came to Him.

30Now Jesus had not yet come into the town, but was in
that place where Martha met Him. 31Then the Jews who were
with her and comforted her in the house, when they saw Mary,
that she rose up hastily and went out, followed her, saying,
"She goes to the grave to weep there."

32Then when Mary had come where Jesus was and saw
Him, she fell down at His feet, saying to Him, "Lord, if You had
been here, my brother would not have died."

33Therefore when Jesus saw her weeping, and the Jews who
came with her also weeping, He groaned in the spirit and was
troubled, 34and said, "Where have you laid him?" They said to
Him, "Lord, come and see."

35Jesus wept. 36Then the Jews said, "Behold how He
loved him!"

[37]And some of them said, "Could not this man, who opened the eyes of the blind, have caused that even this man should not have died?"

[38]Therefore Jesus, again groaning in Himself, came to the grave. It was a cave, and a stone lay on it. [39]Jesus said, "Take away the stone." Martha, the sister of him who was dead, said to Him, "Lord, by this time he stinks, for he has been dead four days."

[40]Jesus said to her, "Did I not say to you that if you would believe you should see the glory of God?"

Observe

Why did Jesus travel to Bethany with His disciples?

....

....

....

How did Mary respond when her sister Martha told her that Jesus wanted to see her?

....

....

....

What did both Martha and Mary say to Jesus when they first saw Him?

....

....

....

JOHN 11:20–40

Interpret

Why did Mary stay in her house as Martha ran to meet with Jesus and talk with Him?

What does Jesus mean when He said to Martha, "I am the resurrection and the life"?

Jesus knew that God would be glorified when He raised Lazarus from the dead, so why did He shed tears that day?

In what ways can you relate with these sisters, especially when Jesus doesn't work on your timeline or in the ways you have asked of Him?

What does the story of Jesus raising Lazarus tell you about how He cares for those He loves?

How is your heart encouraged by this story?

John 11:20–40 Scripture for Memorization/Meditation

"I am the resurrection and the life.
He who believes in Me, though he were
dead, yet shall he live. And whoever lives
and believes in Me shall never die."
VERSES 25–26

Jesus wept.
VERSE 35

Verses for Further Memorization/Meditation

- Trust in Him at all times. You people, pour out your heart before Him. God is a refuge for us (Psalm 62:8).
- For if we have been planted together in the likeness of His death, we shall also be in the likeness of His resurrection, knowing this, that our old man was crucified with Him, that the body of sin might be destroyed, that hereafter we should not serve sin (Romans 6:5–6).
- The LORD is good, a stronghold in the day of trouble, and He knows those who trust in Him (Nahum 1:7).
- "For the eyes of the Lord are on the righteous, and His ears are open to their prayers, but the face of the Lord is against those who do evil" (1 Peter 3:12).

Study 7

LUKE 10:25–37

One day, a lawyer—meaning an expert in the law of Moses and rabbinical law—asked Jesus a question of eternal importance: "What shall I do to inherit eternal life?" When Jesus answered the question with His own question about what was written in the Law, the lawyer answered that he must love God with everything within him and love his neighbor as himself.

This lawyer had some understanding of the Law but fell short of obeying it as God had called him to do. So instead of going his way and living a life of obedience, he attempted to justify himself by narrowly identifying just who his neighbor was. But Jesus wouldn't allow that. With one of His best-known stories, the parable of the good Samaritan, Jesus illustrated what loving our neighbors as ourselves looks like.

Luke 10:25–37 Study Outline

(VERSE 25)	A lawyer's inquiry about eternal life
(VERSES 26–27)	Love God and your neighbor
(VERSE 28)	Right living
(VERSE 29)	A defensive question
(VERSES 30–32)	A story of an injured man ignored
(VERSES 33–35)	The Good Samaritan
(VERSES 36–37)	Jesus' command

PARABLE OF THE GOOD SAMARITAN

25 And, behold, a certain lawyer stood up and tempted Him,
saying, “Master, what shall I do to inherit eternal life?”

26 He said to him, “What is written in the law? How do
you read it?”

27 And he answered and said, “‘You shall love the Lord
your God with all your heart, and with all your soul, and with
all your strength, and with all your mind,’ and ‘your neighbor
as yourself.’ ”

28 And He said to him, “You have answered rightly. Do this
and you shall live.”

29 But he, wanting to justify himself, said to Jesus, “And
who is my neighbor?”

30 And Jesus answered and said, “A certain man went down
from Jerusalem to Jericho, and fell among thieves, who stripped
him of his clothing, and wounded him, and departed, leaving
him half dead. 31 And by chance there came down that way a
certain priest. And when he saw him, he passed by on the other
side. 32 And likewise a Levite, when he was at the place, came
and looked at him and passed by on the other side. 33 But a
certain Samaritan, as he journeyed, came where he was. And
when he saw him, he had compassion on him, 34 and went to
him, and bound up his wounds, pouring in oil and wine, and
sat him on his own beast, and brought him to an inn, and
took care of him. 35 And on the next day, when he departed,
he took out two pence and gave them to the host, and said to
him, ‘Take care of him. And whatever more you spend, when
I come again, I will repay you.’ 36 Now which of these three do
you think was neighbor to him who fell among the thieves?”

37 And he said, “He who showed mercy to him.”

Then said Jesus to him, “Go and do likewise.”

Observe

What did the lawyer ask Jesus? What did He tell the man?

What was the lawyer's understanding of the law of Moses?

Of the three men who saw the wounded traveler left for dead, which one demonstrated true love for his neighbor?

Interpret

When Jesus was on earth, Jews in the land of Israel despised the Samaritans. Why would Jesus make the Samaritan the "good guy" in His parable?

What was the lawyer's motivation when he asked Jesus, "Who is my neighbor?" How did Jesus' response address his true intentions?

What does the Bible mean when it tells us to "show mercy" to those in need?

In your life, who are the "neighbors" God has called you to love? How can you show them love and compassion?

What personal barriers do you battle in demonstrating real love to the less fortunate in our world?

What changes or adjustments might you need to make so you can help others with your resources and time?

Luke 10:25–37 Scripture for Memorization/Meditation

"Now which of these three do you think was
neighbor to him who fell among the thieves?"
And he said, "He who showed mercy to him."
Then said Jesus to him, "Go and do likewise."
VERSES 36–37

Verses for Further Memorization/Meditation

- He has shown you, O man, what is good. And what does the LORD require of you, but to do justice and to love mercy and to walk humbly with your God? (Micah 6:8).
- Put on, therefore, as the elect of God, holy and beloved, hearts of mercies, kindness, humbleness of mind, meekness, long-suffering (Colossians 3:12).
- But the fruit of the Spirit is love, joy, peace, long-suffering, gentleness, goodness, faith, meekness, self-control (Galatians 5:22–23).
- And besides this, giving all diligence, add to your faith, virtue; and to virtue, knowledge; and to knowledge, self-control; and to self-control, patience; and to patience, godliness; and to godliness, brotherly kindness; and to brotherly kindness, love (2 Peter 1:5–7).

Study 8

JOHN 10:22–38

Jesus wasn't the least bit reluctant when it came to declaring who He really was and what that meant. In John 10:22–38, Jesus infuriated the Jewish religious leaders when He asserted that the men who were questioning Him didn't recognize Him as the Messiah, despite all He had said and done, because they weren't among those He treasured as His "sheep."

Then, Jesus sent these men into a murderous rage when He made this astonishing claim: "My Father and I are one." These leaders knew what Jesus was saying, and they picked up rocks to stone Him for blasphemy. But Jesus didn't back down. Instead, He continued calling God "My Father," even telling them, "The Father is in Me and I in Him."

John 10:22–38 Study Outline

(VERSES 22–24) Jesus questioned about His identity

(VERSES 25–30) Jesus states His true identity

(VERSES 31–33) Angry Jews intend to kill Jesus

(VERSES 34–38) Jesus' relationship with God the Father

Jesus Asserts His Deity

[22]And it was the Feast of the Dedication in Jerusalem, and it was winter. [23]And Jesus walked in the temple in Solomon's porch. [24]Then the Jews came around Him and said to Him, "How long do You make us to doubt? If You are the Christ, tell us plainly."

[25]Jesus answered them, "I told you, and you do not believe. The works that I do in My Father's name, they bear witness of Me. [26]But you do not believe because you are not of My sheep, as I said to you. [27]My sheep hear My voice, and I know them, and they follow Me. [28]And I give eternal life to them, and they shall never perish, nor shall any man pluck them out of My hand. [29]My Father, who gave them to Me, is greater than all. And no man is able to pluck them out of My Father's hand. [30]My Father and I are one."

[31]Then the Jews took up stones again to stone Him. [32]Jesus answered them, "I have shown you many good works from My Father. For which of those works do you stone Me?"

[33]The Jews answered Him, saying, "For a good work we do not stone You, but for blasphemy, and because You, being a man, make Yourself God."

[34]Jesus answered them, "Is it not written in your Law, 'I said, "You are gods"?' [35]If He called them gods, to whom the word of God came (and the scripture cannot be broken), [36]do you say of Him whom the Father has sanctified and sent into the world, 'You are blaspheming,' because I said, 'I am the Son of God'? [37]If I do not do the works of My Father, do not believe Me. [38]But if I do, though you do not believe Me, believe the works, that you may know and believe that the Father is in Me and I in Him."

Observe

Where and during what time of year did Jesus talk with the Jewish religious leaders in this passage?

How did Jesus describe Himself that day?

How did the religious leaders react to Jesus' claims? What was His response to their complaints and accusations?

Interpret

What does Jesus say about His relationship with His sheep—and their relationship to Him?

What do you think Jesus meant when He said, "Nor shall any man pluck [My sheep] out of My hand"?

What does "My Father and I are one" really mean?

Apply

Jesus boldly proclaimed His true identity, even when facing the hostility of His enemies. How can you find courage to tell others who Jesus is and what He means to you?

When talking about His sheep, Jesus promised to keep those who belong to Him forever. How does knowing that no one can pluck you out of His hand bring comfort to your heart and confidence to your faith?

How does reading Jesus' words and learning about His earthly ministry through scripture bring encouragement and strengthen your faith?

John 10:22–38 Scripture for Memorization/Meditation

"My Father and I are one."
VERSE 30

"Though you do not believe Me, believe
the works, that you may know and believe
that the Father is in Me and I in Him."
VERSE 38

Verses for Further Memorization/Meditation

- "And no man has ascended up to heaven but He who came down from heaven, even the Son of Man who is in heaven" (John 3:13).
- "Search the scriptures, for in them you think you have eternal life. And these are they that testify of Me" (John 5:39).
- Then Jesus cried out in the temple as He taught, saying, "You both know Me and you know where I am from. And I have not come of Myself, but He who sent me is true, whom you do not know. But I know Him, for I am from Him, and He has sent Me" (John 7:28–29).
- For in Him dwells all the fullness of the Godhead bodily. And you are complete in Him, who is the head of all principality and power (Colossians 2:9–10).

Study 9

MARK 2:1–12

As Jesus taught a large crowd in a house in Capernaum, four men engaged in an incredible act of faith. . .and of heartwarming concern for their paralyzed friend. Rather than waiting for a more convenient time to bring this poor soul to Jesus, the men tore a hole in the roof and lowered their friend to the God-Man he desperately needed to see.

But instead of immediately healing the paralytic, Jesus shook up the religious authorities by saying to the man, "Son, your sins are forgiven." The scribes reasoned in their hearts, *Why does this man speak blasphemies?* Without realizing it, they acknowledged Jesus' authority on earth when they thought, *Who can forgive sins but God alone?*

Jesus came to earth to bring forgiveness and healing to hurting, lost people. That day in Capernaum, He brought both to one paralyzed, sinful man.

Mark 2:1–12 Study Outline

(VERSES 1–2)	Jesus preaches in a home in Capernaum
(VERSES 3–4)	A great act of faith
(VERSE 5)	Jesus forgives the paralytic's sins
(VERSES 6–7)	Jewish religious leaders react to Jesus forgiving sins
(VERSES 8–11)	Jesus asserts His authority to forgive sin
(VERSE 12)	Witnesses glorify God

HEALING AND FORGIVENESS THROUGH JESUS

[1]And again He entered into Capernaum after some days, and it was reported that He was in the house. [2]And immediately many were gathered together, to such an extent that there was no room to receive them, no, not even around the door. And He preached the word to them. [3]And they came to Him, bringing a paralytic who was carried by four men. [4]And when they could not come near to Him because of the crowd, they uncovered the roof where He was. And when they had broken it up, they let down the bed on which the paralytic was lying. [5]When Jesus saw their faith, He said to the paralytic, "Son, your sins are forgiven."

[6]But there were some of the scribes sitting there and reasoning in their hearts, [7]"Why does this man speak blasphemies like this? Who can forgive sins but God alone?"

[8]And immediately, when Jesus perceived in His spirit that they so reasoned within themselves, He said to them, "Why do you reason these things in your hearts? [9]Which is easier, to say to the one who is paralyzed, 'Your sins are forgiven you,' or to say, 'Arise, and take up your bed, and walk'? [10]But so that you may know that the Son of Man has power on earth to forgive sins"—He said to the paralytic—[11]"I say to you, arise, and take up your bed, and go your way to your house."

[12]And immediately he arose, took up the bed, and went out before them all, to such an extent that they were all amazed and glorified God, saying, "We have never seen anything like this."

Observe

What was Jesus doing when the events in this story took place?

What obstacle did the friends of the paralytic face and how did they work around it?

How did Jesus show that He had authority to forgive sins?

Interpret

What do the details of the story tell you about Jesus' reputation?

Why do you think Jesus chose to forgive the man's sins before healing him physically?

How would you contrast Jesus' response to the paralyzed man with the Pharisees' attitudes?

Apply

What are some specific ways you can demonstrate your faith today and every day?

We all have places of brokenness and heartache in life. Where do you need to ask God for healing in yours?

Friendship is a powerful blessing to believers. How can you be the kind of friend who provides meaningful support, just like the ones helping the paralytic?

Mark 2:1–12 Scripture for Memorization/Meditation

"Which is easier, to say to the one who is paralyzed, 'Your sins are forgiven you,' or to say, 'Arise, and take up your bed, and walk'? But so that you may know that the Son of Man has power on earth to forgive sins"—He said to the paralytic—"I say to you, arise, and take up your bed, and go your way to your house."
VERSES 9–11

Verses for Further Memorization/Meditation

- "I, even I, am He who blots out your transgressions for My own sake and will not remember your sins" (Isaiah 43:25).
- We have redemption through His blood, the forgiveness of sins, according to the riches of His grace (Ephesians 1:7).
- I acknowledged my sin to You, and my iniquity I have not hidden. I said, "I will confess my transgressions to the Lord," and You forgave the iniquity of my sin (Psalm 32:5).
- Bless the Lord, O my soul, and do not forget all His benefits, who forgives all your iniquities, who heals all your diseases, who redeems your life from destruction, who crowns you with loving-kindness and tender mercies (Psalm 103:2–4).

Study 10

MATTHEW 14:22–33

Imagine the absolute terror Jesus' disciples must have felt when they saw a lone figure approaching them that stormy night—walking on the water! But also imagine the relief they felt when they heard their Master call out, "Be of good cheer. It is I; do not be afraid."

What followed was Peter—always one to step out while others hung back—passing a test of faith. . .then failing that same test.

The story offers us valuable lessons about faith today—about trusting God wholeheartedly when He says, "Come!" It also teaches us the importance of remaining focused on Jesus when we're surrounded on all sides by frightening difficulties.

Matthew 14:22–33 Study Outline

(VERSES 22–23)	Jesus sends the disciples across the lake while He stays behind to pray
(VERSE 24)	A violent storm arises
(VERSES 25–26)	Jesus walks on the sea, frightening the disciples
(VERSE 27)	Jesus speaks words of comfort
(VERSES 28–30)	With Jesus' permission, Peter walks on the sea, then loses focus, sinks, and is rescued
(VERSE 31)	Jesus rebukes Peter for doubting
(VERSE 32)	Jesus calms the storm
(VERSE 33)	The disciples worship Jesus

Jesus Walks on the Water

22And immediately Jesus compelled His disciples to get into a
ship and to go before Him to the other side, while He sent the
multitudes away. 23And when He had sent the multitudes away,
He went up by Himself on a mountain to pray. And when the
evening came, He was there alone. 24But the ship was now in the
midst of the sea, tossed with waves, for the wind was contrary.

25And in the fourth watch of the night Jesus went to them,
walking on the sea. 26And when the disciples saw Him walking
on the sea, they were troubled, saying, "It is a spirit." And they
cried out in fear.

27But immediately Jesus spoke to them, saying, "Be of good
cheer. It is I; do not be afraid."

28And Peter answered Him and said, "Lord, if it is You, bid
me to come to You on the water."

29And He said, "Come." And when Peter came down out
of the ship, he walked on the water to go to Jesus. 30But when
he saw the wind was boisterous, he was afraid. And beginning
to sink, he cried, saying, "Lord, save me!"

31And immediately Jesus stretched out His hand and caught
him, and said to him, "O you of little faith, why did you doubt?"
32And when they came into the ship, the wind ceased.

33Then those who were in the ship came and worshipped
Him, saying, "Truly You are the Son of God."

Observe

What did Jesus command the disciples to do after He fed the five thousand? What did He do next?

What problem did the disciples face after Jesus sent them on a journey across the lake?

What request did Peter make of Jesus? How did it turn out for him?

Interpret

Why do you think Jesus went out of His way to pray alone? Why did He feel the need to pray at that time?

Why did Jesus send the disciples across the lake, knowing they would face a storm?

In what way did Peter succeed when he first saw Jesus walking on the water? Why did he fail after initially stepping out in faith?

How do you usually react when you find yourself in a situation that creates anxiety and fear?

What does this account teach you about facing dangerous life storms even when you're obeying God?

What lessons can Peter's faith—in spite of his human limitations—teach us?

MATTHEW 14:22–33 SCRIPTURE FOR MEMORIZATION/MEDITATION

But immediately Jesus spoke to them, saying,
"Be of good cheer. It is I; do not be afraid."
VERSE 27

Then those who were in the ship came and worshipped
Him, saying, "Truly You are the Son of God."
VERSE 33

VERSES FOR FURTHER MEMORIZATION/MEDITATION

- And there shall be a tabernacle for shade from the heat in the daytime and a place of refuge and a shelter from storm and from rain (Isaiah 4:6).
- You rule the raging of the sea; when its waves arise, You still them (Psalm 89:9).
- We are troubled on every side, yet not distressed; we are perplexed, but not in despair; persecuted, but not forsaken; thrown down, but not destroyed (2 Corinthians 4:8–9).
- I sought the LORD, and He heard me and delivered me from all my fears (Psalm 34:4).

Study 11

MATTHEW 5:38–48

In His Sermon on the Mount, Jesus delivered some radical teaching as He elaborated on and gave clarity to the law of Moses. His teaching that day was both hard and practical, and it was radically different from anything the people living in the land of Israel had ever heard.

This study, which focuses on Matthew 5:38–48, offers just that kind of teaching. What Jesus taught in this passage goes against all human nature and logic. Don't resist those who deliberately do you wrong? Love those whose attitudes and actions define them as your enemies? Love those who refuse to love you in return? Surely Jesus couldn't have been serious!

Actually, Jesus *was* serious, and He taught that those who do such things mark themselves as true children of the living God.

Matthew 5:38–48 Study Outline

(VERSES 38–39)	Dealing with those who do you wrong
(VERSES 40–41)	A further level of kindness
(VERSE 42)	Giving to those in need
(VERSES 43–45)	Love your enemies
(VERSES 46–47)	A different approach to love
(VERSE 48)	Be imitators of God

Forgiveness and Doing Good for Your Enemies

38“You have heard that it has been said, ‘An eye for an eye and
a tooth for a tooth.’ 39But I say to you, do not resist evil. But
whoever strikes you on your right cheek, turn to him the other
also. 40And if any man sues you in court and takes away your
coat, let him have your cloak also. 41And whoever compels
you to go a mile, go with him two. 42Give to him who asks you,
and do not turn away from him who would borrow from you.

43“You have heard that it has been said, ‘You shall love your
neighbor and hate your enemy.’ 44But I say to you, love your
enemies, bless those who curse you, do good to those who hate
you, and pray for those who despitefully use you and persecute you, 45that you may be the children of your Father who
is in heaven. For He makes His sun to rise on the evil and on
the good, and sends rain on the just and on the unjust. 46For if
you love those who love you, what reward do you have? Don’t
even the tax collectors do the same? 47And if you greet your
brothers only, what do you do more than others? Don’t even
the tax collectors do so? 48Therefore you be perfect, even as
your Father who is in heaven is perfect.”

Observe

What was the setting of Jesus' teaching in Matthew 5:38–48?

In what ways did Jesus tell listeners to love their enemies?

What reward or benefit is there in loving one's enemies?

Interpret

What does it mean to "love your enemies"? What does that kind of love look like?

Where does the phrase "Love your neighbor and hate your enemy" come from?

In what ways did Jesus demonstrate love for His enemies?

Apply

How do people in general love those who love them?

In what specific ways can you show love to people who don't love you back?

How can you possibly "be perfect, even as your Father who is in heaven is perfect"?

Matthew 5:38–48 Scripture for Memorization/Meditation

"You have heard that it has been said, 'You shall love your neighbor and hate your enemy.' But I say to you, love your enemies, bless those who curse you, do good to those who hate you, and pray for those who despitefully use you and persecute you."
VERSES 43–44

"Therefore you be perfect, even as your Father who is in heaven is perfect."
VERSE 48

Verses for Further Memorization/Meditation

- Do not rejoice when your enemy falls, and do not let your heart be glad when he stumbles, lest the LORD see it, and it displease Him, and He turn away His wrath from him (Proverbs 24:17–18).
- "But love your enemies, and do good, and lend, hoping for nothing back. And your reward shall be great, and you shall be the children of the Highest. For He is kind to the unthankful and to the evil" (Luke 6:35).
- Do not repay evil for evil to any man. Provide honest things in the sight of all men. If it is possible, as much as it lies in you, live peaceably with all men. Do not avenge yourselves, dearly beloved, but rather give place to wrath, for it is written, "Vengeance is Mine. I will repay," says the Lord (Romans 12:17–19).

Study 12

MATTHEW 9:9–17

If you were seeking out someone to serve on your staff for a world-changing ministry, it wouldn't be a man like Matthew. Yet that's exactly what Jesus did when He called this man, a tax collector for the Roman government.

To the Jewish people living in the land of Israel, tax collectors were seen as the lowest of the low. They were considered traitors to their own people, and by choosing to even associate with a man like Matthew, Jesus risked putting Himself even more at odds with the Jewish religious leadership of the day.

But Jesus didn't choose Matthew (or any of His followers for that matter) based on their credentials or reputation. He chose His followers, flawed as they were, then made them fit for His service.

Matthew 9:9–17 Study Outline

(VERSE 9)	Jesus' call to "follow"
(VERSES 10–11)	Dining with sinners
(VERSES 12–13)	Calling sinners to repentance
(VERSES 14–17)	New realities in God's kingdom

The Call of Matthew

9And as Jesus passed forth from there, He saw a man named
Matthew sitting at the place where tax was collected. And
He said to him, "Follow Me." And he arose and followed Him.

10And it came to pass, as Jesus sat at the table in the house,
behold, many tax collectors and sinners came and sat down
with Him and His disciples. 11And when the Pharisees saw it,
they said to His disciples, "Why does your Master eat with tax
collectors and sinners?"

12But when Jesus heard that, He said to them, "Those who
are healthy do not need a physician, but those who are sick.
13But go and learn what this means: 'I will have mercy and
not sacrifice.' For I have come to call not the righteous but
sinners to repentance."

14Then the disciples of John came to Him, saying, "Why do
we and the Pharisees fast often, but Your disciples do not fast?"

15And Jesus said to them, "Can the children of the bride-
chamber mourn as long as the bridegroom is with them? But
the days will come when the bridegroom shall be taken from
them, and then they shall fast. 16No man puts a piece of new
cloth on an old garment. For what is put in to fill it up takes
from the garment, and the tear is made worse. 17Nor do men
put new wine into old bottles. Otherwise the bottles break,
and the wine runs out, and the bottles perish. But they put
new wine into new bottles, and both are preserved."

Observe

What was Matthew doing when Jesus called him to "Follow Me"?

....

....

....

....

....

....

What did Jesus do to draw criticism from the Jewish religious leaders?

....

....

....

....

....

....

How did Jesus respond to this criticism?

....

....

....

....

....

....

Interpret

Matthew was a Jew working for the Roman government and therefore seen as a traitor. Why would Jesus call a man like him to be one of His disciples?

What does Jesus' choice to eat with tax collectors and sinners indicate about how we as His followers should relate to the lost?

Why did John the Baptist's disciples question Jesus about His disciples not fasting? What did His response mean?

Apply

What do you do when you struggle to feel worthy of following Jesus?

How do you think Jesus wants you to treat sinners who desperately need Him? Knowing that, what needs to change in your heart and actions?

What are some ways you can train your thoughts and perspectives to better align with God's?

Matthew 9:9–17 Scripture for Memorization/Meditation

But when Jesus heard that, He said to
them, "Those who are healthy do not need
a physician, but those who are sick."
VERSE 12

"But go and learn what this means: 'I will have
mercy and not sacrifice.' For I have come to call
not the righteous but sinners to repentance."
VERSE 13

Verses for Further Memorization/Meditation

- For I am the least of the apostles, and am not suitable to be called an apostle, because I persecuted the church of God. But by the grace of God I am what I am, and His grace that was bestowed on me was not in vain (1 Corinthians 15:9–10).
- When Simon Peter saw it, he fell down at Jesus' knees, saying, "Depart from me, for I am a sinful man, O Lord" (Luke 5:8).
- God has chosen the foolish things of the world to confound the wise, and God has chosen the weak things of the world to confound the things that are mighty. And God has chosen lowly things of the world and things that are despised (1 Corinthians 1:27–28).

Study 13

LUKE 11:1–13

The disciples had just watched their Master as He prayed, and it stirred something inside them; they wanted to know how He prayed with such power and how He bound His heart and mind to His Father. *How can we pray like Him?* they wondered. But more importantly, they opened their mouths and made this request: "Lord, teach us to pray."

Jesus was happy to answer such a request. He spoke to them what we today know as "the Lord's Prayer," not necessarily so they could recite it word for word, but so they could model their own prayers after it. What's more, Jesus taught His disciples the importance of persistence in prayer and God's willingness to honor and answer such prayers with His very best.

Luke 11:1–13 Study Outline

(VERSE 1)	How should we pray?
(VERSES 2–4)	The model prayer
(VERSES 5–8)	Persistent prayer
(VERSES 9–10)	Ask, seek, knock
(VERSES 11–13)	A perfect God gives perfect gifts

Jesus' Teaching on Prayer

1 And it came to pass, that, as He was praying in a certain place, when He ceased, one of His disciples said to Him, "Lord, teach us to pray, as John also taught his disciples."

> 2 And He said to them, "When you pray, say:
> Our Father who is in heaven,
> Hallowed be Your name.
> Your kingdom come.
> Your will be done, as in heaven, so on earth.
> 3 Give us day by day our daily bread.
> 4 And forgive us our sins,
> for we also forgive everyone who is indebted to us.
> And do not lead us into temptation,
> but deliver us from evil."

5 And He said to them, "Which of you shall have a friend, and shall go to him at midnight and say to him, 'Friend, lend me three loaves, 6 for a friend of mine has come to me in his journey, and I have nothing to set before him'; 7 and from within he shall answer and say, 'Do not trouble me; the door is now shut, and my children are with me in bed; I cannot rise and give you anything'? 8 I say to you, though he will not rise and give to him because he is his friend, yet because of his persistence he will rise and give him as many as he needs. 9 And I say to you, ask, and it shall be given to you; seek, and you shall find; knock, and it shall be opened to you. 10 For everyone who asks receives, and he who seeks finds, and to him who knocks it shall be opened. 11 If a son asks for bread from any of you who is a father, will he give him a stone? Or if he asks for a fish, will he give him a serpent instead of a fish? 12 Or if he asks for an egg, will he offer him a scorpion? 13 If you then, being evil, know how to give good gifts to your children, how much more shall your heavenly Father give the Holy Spirit to those who ask Him?"

Observe

What request did the disciples make of Jesus in verse 1?

What do the first few lines of the Lord's Prayer say about the way we should address God when we pray?

What are the basic elements of prayer listed in this passage?

Interpret

Why is it important to address God as "Our Father"?

What do verses 9–10 tell us about God's desire to hear and answer our prayers?

What do verses 11–13 tell us about the heart of God for His people?

Apply

How convinced are you that God really wants you to pray to Him? Why?

How have you used the Lord's Prayer in your own prayer life? What influence has it had?

What exactly do verses 9–10 mean in your life? How do these words affect your faith and emotions?

LUKE 11:1–13 SCRIPTURE FOR MEMORIZATION/MEDITATION

"And I say to you, ask, and it shall be given to you; seek, and you shall find; knock, and it shall be opened to you. For everyone who asks receives, and he who seeks finds, and to him who knocks it shall be opened."
VERSES 9–10

"If you then, being evil, know how to give good gifts to your children, how much more shall your heavenly Father give the Holy Spirit to those who ask Him?"
VERSE 13

VERSES FOR FURTHER MEMORIZATION/MEDITATION

- For there is not a word on my tongue, but behold, O LORD, You know it altogether (Psalm 139:4).
- And this is the confidence that we have in Him, that if we ask anything according to His will, He hears us. And if we know that He hears us, whatever we ask, we know that we have the petitions that we desired from Him (1 John 5:14–15).
- "For the eyes of the Lord are on the righteous, and His ears are open to their prayers, but the face of the Lord is against those who do evil" (1 Peter 3:12).
- Be anxious for nothing, but in everything, by prayer and supplication with thanksgiving, let your requests be made known to God. And the peace of God, which passes all understanding, shall guard your hearts and minds through Christ Jesus (Philippians 4:6–7).

Study 14

JOHN 15:1–14

When Jesus spoke of Himself as "the true vine" and His disciples as "the branches," He was using a symbol the disciples would have clearly understood. The Hebrew scriptures (the Old Testament) repeatedly used this imagery to illustrate the relationship between God and His people (see Psalm 80:8–9, for example). Also, grapevines were everywhere in the land of Israel, giving the disciples a visual example of what Jesus was to be to His people.

Jesus wanted these men, who would soon begin taking the gospel message into the world around them, to be completely dependent upon and rooted in Him. When they were, they could receive the spiritual sustenance and power they would need to accomplish great things (in other words, bear fruit) for Him.

John 15:1–14 Study Outline

(VERSE 1)	The true vine
(VERSES 2–8)	Abiding in the true vine
(VERSES 9–11)	Obedience, love, and joy
(VERSE 12)	Love one another
(VERSES 13–14)	The greatest love

THE VINE AND THE BRANCHES

[1]"I am the true vine, and My Father is the vinedresser. [2]Every
branch in Me that does not bear fruit He takes away, and every
branch that bears fruit He purges, that it may bring forth more
fruit. [3]Now you are clean through the word that I have spoken
to you. [4]Abide in Me, and I in you. As the branch cannot bear
fruit by itself, unless it abides in the vine, no more can you,
unless you abide in Me.

[5]"I am the vine; you are the branches. He who abides in
Me, and I in him, the same brings forth much fruit. For without
Me you can do nothing. [6]If a man does not abide in Me, he is
cast forth as a branch and is withered, and men gather them
and cast them into the fire, and they are burned. [7]If you abide
in Me, and My words abide in you, you shall ask what you will,
and it shall be done for you. [8]In this My Father is glorified, that
you bear much fruit; so you shall be My disciples.

[9]"As the Father has loved Me, so have I loved you; continue
in My love. [10]If you keep My commandments, you shall abide
in My love, even as I have kept My Father's commandments
and abide in His love. [11]These things I have spoken to you,
that My joy might remain in you, and that your joy might be
full. [12]This is My commandment, that you love one another
as I have loved you. [13]No man has greater love than this, that
a man lay down his life for his friends. [14]You are My friends if
you do whatever I command you."

Observe

How does Jesus describe His relationship with us and our relationship to Him?

What three conditions did Jesus give for receiving something from God?

What makes us friends of Jesus? How do we remain in Christ's love?

JOHN 15:1–14

Interpret

What does it mean to "abide" in Jesus?

What are the benefits of abiding in Him?

What should mark or define the relationship between followers of Christ?

Apply

How can you know with confidence that you are attached to the vine?

What practical steps can you take every day to abide in Jesus?

Why is it important that we deliberately remain close to Jesus Christ? What happens if we don't?

John 15:1–14 Scripture for Memorization/Meditation

"Abide in Me, and I in you. As the branch cannot bear fruit by itself, unless it abides in the vine, no more can you, unless you abide in Me. I am the vine; you are the branches. He who abides in Me, and I in him, the same brings forth much fruit. For without Me you can do nothing."

VERSES 4–5

"As the Father has loved Me, so have I loved you; continue in My love. If you keep My commandments, you shall abide in My love, even as I have kept My Father's commandments and abide in His love."

VERSES 9–10

Verses for Further Memorization/Meditation

- But whoever keeps His word, truly the love of God is perfected in him. By this we know that we are in Him: he who says he abides in Him ought himself also to walk even as He walked (1 John 2:5–6).
- "My sheep hear My voice, and I know them, and they follow Me. And I give eternal life to them, and they shall never perish, nor shall any man pluck them out of My hand" (John 10:27–28).
- Whoever abides in Him does not sin. Whoever sins has not seen Him or known Him (1 John 3:6).

Study 15

JOHN 14:15–27

The first fourteen verses of John 14 recount Jesus' words of comfort and encouragement for His disciples as He prepared them for His departure from this world. But Jesus wouldn't leave them alone to fend for themselves. No, He would ask His Father to send them a comforter—the Holy Spirit, who would work within them to comfort them, teach them, and remind them of everything He had taught them over the previous three years.

The Holy Spirit continues that same work—and more—in our lives today. He comforts, guides, strengthens, and encourages each person whose faith is in Jesus and who has acknowledged Him as Lord over their lives.

John 14:15–27 Study Outline

(VERSE 15) Evidence of believers' love for Jesus

(VERSES 16–18) The promised comforter

(VERSES 19–21) Wonderful promises of God's love

(VERSES 22–24) Obedience and love

(VERSES 25–27) Comfort and peace

Jesus Promises the Holy Spirit

15“If you love Me, keep My commandments. 16And I will pray
to the Father, and He shall give you another Comforter, that
He may abide with you forever— 17even the Spirit of truth,
whom the world cannot receive, because it does not see Him,
nor does it know Him. But you know Him, for He dwells with
you and shall be in you. 18I will not leave you comfortless; I
will come to you.

19“Yet a little while, and the world will see Me no more,
but you see Me. Because I live, you shall live also. 20On that
day you shall know that I am in My Father, and you in Me, and
I in you. 21He who has My commandments and keeps them, it
is he who loves Me. And he who loves Me shall be loved by
My Father, and I will love him, and will reveal Myself to him.”

22Judas (not Iscariot) said to Him, “Lord, how is it that You
will reveal Yourself to us and not to the world?”

23Jesus answered and said to him, “If a man loves Me, he
will keep My words, and My Father will love him, and We will
come to him and make Our dwelling with him. 24He who does
not love Me does not keep My sayings, and the word that you
hear is not Mine but the Father’s who sent Me.

25“These things I have spoken to you, being yet present
with you. 26But the Comforter, who is the Holy Spirit, whom
the Father will send in My name, He shall teach you all things
and bring to your remembrance all things that I have said to
you. 27I leave peace with you; I give to you My peace. I do not
give to you as the world gives.”

Observe

What various names does Jesus give to God's Spirit in this passage?

Why can only those who know and love Jesus receive the Holy Spirit?

What other roles did Jesus say the Holy Spirit would play in the lives of believers?

JOHN 14:15–27

Interpret

Read John 16:5–15. What had to happen before God sent the Holy Spirit?

How is the peace of Jesus different from the peace of this world?

Where is the Holy Spirit today?

Apply

How should you demonstrate your faithful love for Jesus?

In what ways does God's Spirit within you bring comfort?

How does being a spirit-filled and spirit-led believer positively affect how you live and think each day?

John 14:15–27 Scripture for Memorization/Meditation

"If you love Me, keep My commandments."
VERSE 15

"But the Comforter, who is the Holy Spirit, whom the Father will send in My name, He shall teach you all things and bring to your remembrance all things that I have said to you."
VERSE 26

Verses for Further Memorization/Meditation

- Now may the God of hope fill you with all joy and peace in believing, that you may abound in hope through the power of the Holy Spirit (Romans 15:13).
- Do you not know that your body is the temple of the Holy Spirit, who is in you, whom you have from God, and you are not your own? (1 Corinthians 6:19).
- Then Peter said to them, "Repent, and every one of you be baptized in the name of Jesus Christ for the remission of sins, and you shall receive the gift of the Holy Spirit" (Acts 2:38).
- Likewise the Spirit also helps our infirmities. For we do not know what we should pray for as we ought, but the Spirit Himself makes intercession for us with groanings that cannot be uttered (Romans 8:26).

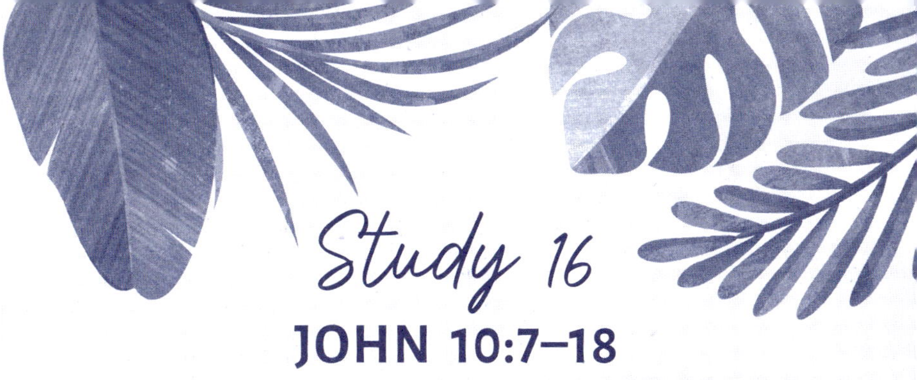

Study 16

JOHN 10:7–18

People living in the land of Israel were familiar with the work of shepherds. They knew that these men led their sheep to necessary food and water while protecting them from predators—both human thieves and wild animals that would kill and eat them.

When Jesus identified Himself as "the good shepherd," He was letting His followers know that He was no ordinary caretaker. Shepherds were dedicated to providing for and protecting their flocks, but they were typically hired hands who would hardly imperil themselves for the sheep. Jesus, on the other hand, is the good shepherd who "gives His life for the sheep." He is the shepherd who knows His sheep intimately. In return, they know Him, hear His voice, and willingly follow Him.

John 10:7–18 Study Outline

(VERSES 7–10)	The door of the sheep
(VERSES 11–13)	The good shepherd who gives His life for His sheep
(VERSES 14–15)	The good shepherd who knows His sheep
(VERSE 16)	Other sheep
(VERSES 17–18)	Sacrificial, obedient love

The Good Shepherd

7Then Jesus said to them again, “Truly, truly, I say to you, I am
the door of the sheep. 8All who ever came before Me are thieves
and robbers, but the sheep did not hear them. 9I am the door.
If any man enters in by Me, he shall be saved and shall go in
and out and find pasture. 10The thief does not come except to
steal and to kill and to destroy. I have come that they might
have life, and that they might have it more abundantly.

11“I am the good shepherd. The good shepherd gives His
life for the sheep. 12But he who is a hired hand, and not the
shepherd, who does not own the sheep, sees the wolf coming
and leaves the sheep and flees. And the wolf catches them
and scatters the sheep. 13The hired hand flees because he is a
hired hand and does not care for the sheep.

14“I am the good shepherd, and know My sheep, and am
known by My own. 15As the Father knows Me, even so I know
the Father, and I lay down My life for the sheep. 16And I have
other sheep that are not of this fold. I must bring them also,
and they shall hear My voice. And there shall be one fold and
one shepherd. 17Therefore My Father loves Me, because I lay
down My life that I might take it again. 18No man takes it from
Me, but I lay it down of Myself. I have power to lay it down,
and I have power to take it again. This commandment I have
received from My Father.”

Observe

How does Jesus describe Himself in this passage?

How is our heavenly good shepherd different from literal earthly shepherds?

What does Jesus repeatedly say He will do for His sheep?

JOHN 10:7–18

Interpret

Who are the sheep Jesus refers to in this passage?

What did Jesus mean when He said He would lay down His life for His sheep?

Who are the "other sheep" Jesus spoke of in verse 16?

Apply

JOHN 10:7–18

In what ways do you see Jesus as the good shepherd in your life? What benefits does that bring?

Do you find it easy or hard to fully trust Jesus as the "good shepherd"? Why?

What do you think the "abundant life" Jesus mentioned in verse 10 looks like? Are you living an abundant life today?

John 10:7–18 Scripture for Memorization/Meditation

"The thief does not come except to steal and to kill and to destroy. I have come that they might have life, and that they might have it more abundantly."
VERSE 10

"I am the good shepherd. The good shepherd gives His life for the sheep."
VERSE 11

Verses for Further Memorization/Meditation

- Like a shepherd, He shall feed His flock. He shall gather the lambs with His arm and carry them in His bosom, and shall gently lead those who are with young (Isaiah 40:11).
- Now may the God of peace, who brought again from the dead our Lord Jesus, that great Shepherd of the sheep, through the blood of the everlasting covenant, make you perfect in every good work to do His will, working in you what is well pleasing in His sight, through Jesus Christ, to whom be glory forever and ever. Amen (Hebrews 13:20–21).
- For you were as sheep going astray but are now returned to the Shepherd and Bishop of your souls (1 Peter 2:25).

Study 17

MATTHEW 9:18–33

This passage is an account of some of Jesus' most amazing miracles—remarkable if for no other reason than that they demonstrated His deep compassion for the sick, the infirmed, the grieving, and the demon possessed.

Jesus showed His authority over disease and evil spirits, as well as His willingness to respond to people's faith. And Jesus demonstrated Himself as the always compassionate Son of God who had come to earth to serve and save.

The healing of a man possessed by an evil spirit that rendered him mute astonished the multitudes who witnessed this miracle. They exclaimed, "This has never been seen in Israel."

Matthew 9:18–33 Study Outline

(verses 18–19) Jesus' response to a ruler's great faith

(verses 20–22) Jesus heals a woman of great faith

(verses 23–26) Jesus raises a girl from the dead

(verses 27–31) Healing two blind men

(verses 32–33) Healing a demon-possessed man

A Series of Miracles

18While He spoke these things to them, behold, there came a certain ruler and worshipped Him, saying, “My daughter is even now dead, but come and lay Your hand on her and she shall live.” 19And Jesus arose and followed him, and so did His disciples.

20And behold, a woman who was diseased twelve years with an issue of blood came behind Him and touched the hem of His garment. 21For she said to herself, “If I can but touch His garment, I shall be healed.”

22But Jesus turned around, and when He saw her, He said, “Daughter, be of good comfort; your faith has healed you.” And the woman was healed from that hour.

23And when Jesus came into the ruler’s house and saw the minstrels and the people making noise, 24He said to them, “Leave, for the maid is not dead, but sleeping.” And they laughed Him to scorn. 25But when the people were sent out, He went in and took her by the hand, and the maid arose. 26And the news of this went out into all that land.

27And when Jesus departed from there, two blind men followed Him, crying and saying, “Son of David, have mercy on us.” 28And when He had come into the house, the blind men came to Him. And Jesus said to them, “Do you believe that I am able to do this?” They said to Him, “Yes, Lord.”

29Then He touched their eyes, saying, “According to your faith let it be done to you.” 30And their eyes were opened. And Jesus strictly charged them, saying, “See that no man knows it.” 31But they, when they had departed, spread the news about Him in all that country.

32As they went out, behold, they brought to Him a mute man possessed with a demon. 33And when the demon was cast out, the mute man spoke. And the multitudes marveled, saying, “This has never been seen in Israel.”

Observe

How many miracles do you see in this short passage? What are they?

In verse 18, who interrupted Jesus as He was speaking and what was his request? How did Jesus respond to his faith?

Who came up behind Jesus as He was walking, and what did she do to receive healing? What was the result?

Interpret

How did Jesus respond to needy people's faith in this passage?

What does this passage show about what is important to Jesus?

What do these miracles say about who Jesus really is?

How does reading this passage encourage your faith and your willingness to ask Jesus to do the impossible?

Why is it important to pray not only for yourself but also for your family and friends?

Where have you seen God work a miracle of healing, restoration, provision, or forgiveness in your life or in the life of someone you love? How does that grow your confidence that He still works miracles today?

Matthew 9:18–33 Scripture for Memorization/Meditation

And when He had come into the house, the blind men came to Him. And Jesus said to them, "Do you believe that I am able to do this?" They said to Him, "Yes, Lord." Then He touched their eyes, saying, "According to your faith let it be done to you." And their eyes were opened.

VERSES 28–30

Verses for Further Memorization/Meditation

- We walk by faith, not by sight (2 Corinthians 5:7).
- Trust in the Lord with all your heart and do not lean on your own understanding. In all your ways acknowledge Him, and He shall direct your paths (Proverbs 3:5–6).
- Jesus said to him, "If you can believe, all things are possible to him who believes" (Mark 9:23).
- Above all, taking the shield of faith, with which you shall be able to quench all the fiery darts of the wicked (Ephesians 6:16).

Study 18

JOHN 20:1–18

Mary Magdalene, one of several women who followed Jesus during His ministry on earth, was among the heartbroken, grieving, and dispirited followers who witnessed their Master's death on a Roman cross. Jesus had cleansed Mary of seven tormenting spirits, and she then followed Him faithfully. Now, the grieving woman's day was made worse when everything she observed led her to the terrible conclusion that someone had stolen Jesus' body.

But then Mary heard the voice of her Lord calling her name. It was Jesus, alive again! And He was about to show Himself before His other heartsick followers in coming days.

John 20:1–18 Study Outline

(VERSES 1–2)	Mary finds the stone rolled away from the sepulchre and runs to tell Peter and John
(VERSES 3–5)	Peter and John run to the sepulchre and peer inside
(VERSES 6–9)	The disciples enter the sepulchre and find Jesus' burial clothes but no body
(VERSE 10)	The disciples return to their homes, leaving Mary behind
(VERSES 11–13)	Mary sees angels inside the tomb
(VERSES 14–15)	The living Savior approaches Mary
(VERSES 16–17)	Mary recognizes Jesus
(VERSES 18)	Mary Magdalene's announcement

THE RISEN JESUS

1The first day of the week Mary Magdalene came to the sepulchre early, when it was still dark, and saw the stone taken away
from the sepulchre. 2Then she ran and came to Simon Peter
and to the other disciple, whom Jesus loved, and said to them,
"They have taken away the Lord out of the sepulchre, and we
do not know where they have laid Him."

3Therefore Peter and that other disciple went out and
went to the sepulchre. 4So they both ran together, and the
other disciple outran Peter and came to the sepulchre first.
5And he, stooping down and looking in, saw the linen cloths
lying there, yet he did not go in. 6Then Simon Peter came,
following him, and went into the sepulchre and saw the linen
cloths lying there, 7and the cloth that was around His head
not lying with the linen cloths but wrapped together in a
place by itself. 8Then that other disciple, who came first to
the sepulchre, also went in, and he saw and believed. 9For as
yet they did not know the scripture, that He must rise again
from the dead. 10Then the disciples went away again to their
own homes.

11But Mary stood outside the sepulchre weeping, and as
she wept she stooped down and looked into the sepulchre.
12And she saw two angels in white sitting, the one at the head
and the other at the feet, where the body of Jesus had lain.
13And they said to her, "Woman, why are you weeping?" She
said to them, "Because they have taken away my Lord, and I
do not know where they have laid Him."

14And when she had said this, she turned herself back and
saw Jesus standing there, and did not know that it was Jesus.
15Jesus said to her, "Woman, why are you weeping? Whom
do you seek?" Supposing Him to be the gardener, she said to
Him, "Sir, if You have carried Him from here, tell me where
You have laid Him, and I will take Him away."

[16]Jesus said to her, "Mary." She turned herself and said to Him, "Rabboni" (which is to say, Master).

[17]Jesus said to her, "Do not touch Me, for I have not yet ascended to My Father, but go to My brothers and say to them, 'I am ascending to My Father and your Father, and to My God and your God.'"

[18]Mary Magdalene came and told the disciples that she had seen the Lord and that He had spoken these things to her.

Observe

What did Mary find when she arrived at Jesus' burial site? What did she do next?

....

....

....

What did the disciples do when Mary told them what she saw?

....

....

....

What happened to Mary after the disciples returned home?

....

....

....

....

Interpret

Why did Mary see the angels, but Peter and John didn't?

Why would the angels ask Mary, "Woman, why are you weeping?"

Why didn't Mary recognize Jesus standing before her until He said her name?

Imagine being in Mary's position. How would you respond to meeting the risen Jesus?

Read Matthew 28:1–11, Mark 16:1–13, and Luke 24:1–12. How are the accounts alike? How are they different? Why?

How does this powerful event affect your daily life?

John 20:1–18 Scripture for Memorization/Meditation

Jesus said to her, "Woman, why are you weeping? Whom do you seek?" Supposing Him to be the gardener, she said to Him, "Sir, if You have carried Him from here, tell me where You have laid Him, and I will take Him away." Jesus said to her, "Mary." She turned herself and said to Him, "Rabboni" (which is to say, Master).
VERSES 15–16

Verses for Further Memorization/Meditation

- Blessed be the God and Father of our Lord Jesus Christ, who according to His abundant mercy has begotten us again to a living hope through the resurrection of Jesus Christ from the dead (1 Peter 1:3).
- But if the Spirit of Him who raised up Jesus from the dead dwells in you, He who raised up Christ from the dead shall also revive your mortal bodies by His Spirit who dwells in you (Romans 8:11).
- And God both raised up the Lord and will also raise us up by His own power (1 Corinthians 6:14).
- That I may know Him and the power of His resurrection and the fellowship of His sufferings, being made conformable to His death, if by any means I might attain to the resurrection of the dead (Philippians 3:10–11).

Study 19

MATTHEW 18:21–35

Forgiveness is a huge deal to God—so big that He sent His Son, Jesus Christ, to earth to live a sinless life before willingly dying a sacrificial death on the cross. Jesus' sacrifice allowed sinful men and women to be forgiven and welcomed into God's eternal kingdom.

But the importance of forgiveness doesn't stop there. In Matthew 18:23–34, Jesus speaks a parable that warns His followers to forgive those who sin against them—to forgive their offenders—from their hearts.

This is a radical forgiveness that chooses to release others from the guilt of their offenses, completely, repeatedly, and without reservation—the same way our Father in heaven has forgiven us.

Matthew 18:21–35 Study Outline

(verse 21)	Peter's question
(verse 22)	Jesus' answer
(verses 23–34)	Parable of the unmerciful servant
(verse 35)	Jesus' warning

The Law of Forgiveness

21 Then Peter came to Him and said, "Lord, how often shall my
brother sin against me and I forgive him? Up to seven times?"

22 Jesus said to him, "I do not say to you, up to seven
times, but up to seventy times seven. 23 Therefore the kingdom of heaven is compared to a certain king who would
take account of his servants. 24 And when he had begun to
settle the accounts, one was brought to him who owed him
ten thousand talents. 25 But since he could not pay, his lord
commanded him to be sold—and his wife, and children, and
all that he had—and payment to be made. 26 Therefore the
servant fell down and worshipped him, saying, 'Lord, have
patience with me, and I will pay you all.' 27 Then the lord of
that servant was moved with compassion and released him
and forgave him the debt.

28 "But the same servant went out and found one of his
fellow servants who owed him a hundred pence. And he
laid hands on him and took him by the throat, saying, 'Pay
me what you owe.' 29 And his fellow servant fell down at his
feet and begged him, saying, 'Have patience with me, and I
will pay you all.' 30 And he would not, but went and cast him
into prison until he should pay the debt. 31 So when his fellow
servants saw what was done, they were very sorry, and came
and told to their lord all that had been done. 32 Then his lord,
after he had called him, said to him, 'O you wicked servant. I
forgave you all that debt because you asked me. 33 Should you
not also have had compassion on your fellow servant, even
as I had pity on you?' 34 And his lord was angry and delivered
him to the tormentors until he should pay all that was due to
him. 35 So likewise shall My heavenly Father do also to every
one of you if you do not forgive your brother his trespasses
from your heart."

Observe

What did Peter ask Jesus about forgiving someone who had sinned against him?

Who are the main characters in this parable of the unmerciful servant? What are the debts owed and to whom?

What are the similarities and differences between the two servants in this parable? How did the master deal with the servant who refused to extend mercy?

Interpret

What does Peter's question reveal about his view of forgiveness?

What did Jesus mean when He told Peter he should forgive "up to seventy times seven"?

Who does the king in this parable represent? What do we learn about him as we read?

Apply

What makes it difficult for you to forgive someone who has wronged you?

How does knowing that God has extended undeserved mercy and forgiveness to you affect your willingness of forgiving others?

To whom do you need to extend mercy and forgiveness? How can you take that next step today?

Matthew 18:21–35 Scripture for Memorization/Meditation

Then Peter came to Him and said, "Lord, how often shall my brother sin against me and I forgive him? Up to seven times?" Jesus said to him, "I do not say to you, up to seven times, but up to seventy times seven."
VERSES 21–22

Verses for Further Memorization/Meditation

- "And when you stand praying, forgive, if you have anything against anyone, that your Father who is in heaven may also forgive you for your trespasses. But if you do not forgive, neither will your Father who is in heaven forgive your trespasses" (Mark 11:25–26).
- Put on, therefore, as the elect of God, holy and beloved, hearts of mercies, kindness, humbleness of mind, meekness, long-suffering, being patient with one another and forgiving one another if any man has a quarrel against any. Even as Christ forgave you, so you also do (Colossians 3:12–13).
- He who covers a transgression seeks love, but he who repeats a matter separates friends (Proverbs 17:9).
- For as the heaven is high above the earth, so great is His mercy toward those who fear Him. As far as the east is from the west, so far has He removed our transgressions from us (Psalm 103:11–12).

Study 20

MATTHEW 6:19–34

In Matthew 6:19–34, Jesus taught an eternal perspective on earthly possessions. He also wanted His followers to know how to approach their basic needs, such as food and clothing. He wasn't saying that working hard to provide for ourselves and our families is wrong in and of itself—the Bible is clear that God honors and blesses hard work. But He did point out that our hearts should be focused on God's eternal kingdom and the treasures awaiting us there.

Earthly treasure is temporary and will most certainly fade away, but our heavenly wealth is secure forever. Not only that, but God is also aware of our needs here on earth and has promised to provide for us.

MATTHEW 6:19–34 STUDY OUTLINE

(VERSES 19–21)	A heavenly focus
(VERSES 22–23)	Judging our eyesight
(VERSES 24)	Serving two masters
(VERSES 25–32)	Don't worry—trust God
(VERSES 33–34)	Seek God's kingdom first

Treasure in Heaven

19“Do not lay up for yourselves treasures on earth, where moth
and rust corrupt, and where thieves break in and steal. 20But lay
up for yourselves treasures in heaven, where neither moth nor
rust corrupts, and where thieves do not break in or steal. 21For
where your treasure is, there your heart will be also.

22“The eye is the light of the body. Therefore if your eye is
healthy, your whole body shall be full of light. 23But if your eye
is evil, your whole body shall be full of darkness. Therefore if
the light that is in you is darkness, how great is that darkness!

24“No man can serve two masters, for either he will hate
the one and love the other, or else he will hold to the one and
despise the other. You cannot serve God and riches.

25“Therefore I say to you, do not worry for your life, what
you shall eat or what you shall drink, or yet for your body, what
you shall put on. Isn’t life more than food and the body more
than clothing? 26Behold the fowls of the air, for they do not
sow; they neither reap nor gather into barns. Yet your heavenly
Father feeds them. Aren’t you much more valuable than they are?
27Which of you by worrying can add one cubit to his stature?

28“And why do you worry about clothing? Consider the lilies
of the field, how they grow: they do not toil, nor do they spin,
29and yet I say to you that even Solomon in all his glory was not
arrayed like one of these. 30Therefore, if God so clothes the grass
of the field, which is here today and tomorrow is cast into the
oven, shall He not much more clothe you, O you of little faith?

31“Therefore do not worry, saying, ‘What shall we eat?’
or ‘What shall we drink?’ or ‘With what shall we be clothed?’
32For the Gentiles seek after all these things. For your heavenly
Father knows that you have need of all these things. 33But seek
first the kingdom of God and His righteousness, and all these
things shall be added to you. 34Therefore don’t worry about
tomorrow, for tomorrow shall worry about its own things. The
day has enough of its own evil.”

MATTHEW 6:19–34

Observe

What does Jesus tell us to focus on while living on this earth?

How does Jesus instruct believers to overcome worry in this life?

What should believers focus on instead of worrying about temporal needs?

Interpret

Why is it impossible to serve God and riches?

Why, according to Jesus, is it foolish to worry about our physical and personal needs?

How are Christians' ambitions and focus to be different from those of non-Christians?

What are some earthly things you treasure? How can you keep these things in their proper place rather than allowing them to trump the eternal?

What worries and fears do you hold on to daily, and how do they affect your relationship with Jesus?

What can you do to replace worry about your earthly needs with unshakable trust that God will always provide at the right time and in the right ways?

Matthew 6:19–34 Scripture for Memorization/Meditation

"Do not lay up for yourselves treasures on earth, where moth and rust corrupt, and where thieves break in and steal. But lay up for yourselves treasures in heaven, where neither moth nor rust corrupts, and where thieves do not break in or steal. For where your treasure is, there your heart will be also."
VERSES 19–21

"Seek first the kingdom of God and His righteousness, and all these things shall be added to you."
VERSE 33

Verses for Further Memorization/Meditation

- God is able to make all grace abound toward you, that always having all sufficiency in all things, you may abound to every good work (2 Corinthians 9:8).
- But my God shall supply all your need according to His riches in glory by Christ Jesus (Philippians 4:19).
- "Are not five sparrows sold for two farthings? And not one of them is forgotten before God. But even the very hairs of your head are all numbered. Therefore do not fear. You are of more value than many sparrows" (Luke 12:6–7).
- Let your conduct be without covetousness, and be content with what you have, for He has said, "I will never leave you or forsake you" (Hebrews 13:5).

Study 21

JOHN 3:1–21

In the still and quiet of the night, a Jewish religious leader named Nicodemus visited with Jesus to talk about eternal matters. Did Nicodemus come to Jesus by night out of fear for how his fellow religious leaders would react? Perhaps. But in seeking out Jesus and asking Him honest questions, Nicodemus received life-changing insights into what it takes for a person to inherit eternal life and the part Jesus played in that process.

In verses 16–18, Jesus spoke a nutshell version of the gospel message, stating plainly that the Father sent Him to earth so people could be saved through faith in Him.

John 3:1–21 Study Outline

(VERSES 1–2)	Nicodemus, a ruler of the Jews
(VERSES 3–4)	People must be born again
(VERSES 5–8)	Born of water and the Spirit
(VERSES 9–15)	Jesus explains why God sent Him
(VERSES 16–21)	God's plan for salvation

The New Birth

1There was a man of the Pharisees named Nicodemus, a ruler
of the Jews. 2The same came to Jesus by night and said to Him,
"Rabbi, we know that You are a teacher come from God. For no
man can do these miracles that You do unless God is with him."

3Jesus answered and said to him, "Truly, truly, I say to you,
unless a man is born again, he cannot see the kingdom of God."

4Nicodemus said to Him, "How can a man be born when
he is old? Can he enter a second time into his mother's womb
and be born?"

5Jesus answered, "Truly, truly, I say to you, unless a man
is born of water and of the Spirit, he cannot enter into the
kingdom of God. 6What is born of the flesh is flesh, and what
is born of the Spirit is spirit. 7Do not marvel that I said to you,
'You must be born again.' 8The wind blows where it wishes, and
you hear the sound of it but cannot tell where it comes from
and where it goes. So is everyone who is born of the Spirit."

9Nicodemus answered and said to Him, "How can these
things be?"

10Jesus answered and said to him, "Are you a master of
Israel and do not know these things? 11Truly, truly, I say to
you, we speak of what we do know and testify of what we have
seen, and you do not receive our testimony. 12If I have told you
earthly things and you do not believe, how shall you believe if I
tell you of heavenly things? 13And no man has ascended up to
heaven but He who came down from heaven, even the Son of
Man who is in heaven. 14And as Moses lifted up the serpent in
the wilderness, even so the Son of Man must be lifted up, 15that
whoever believes in Him should not perish but have eternal life.

16"For God so loved the world that He gave His only
begotten Son, that whoever believes in Him should not
perish but have everlasting life. 17For God did not send His
Son into the world to condemn the world but that the world

might be saved through Him. [18]He who believes in Him is
not condemned, but he who does not believe is condemned
already because he has not believed in the name of the only
begotten Son of God. [19]And this is the condemnation, that
light has come into the world, and men loved darkness rather
than light, because their deeds were evil. [20]For everyone who
does evil hates the light and does not come to the light, lest
his deeds should be exposed. [21]But he who does truth comes
to the light, that his deeds may be revealed, that they are
worked in God."

Observe

Who was Nicodemus? What important group was he a part of?

How does Nicodemus greet Jesus as their conversation begins?

Why must a person be born again?

Interpret

Why would Nicodemus visit Jesus at night?

What are the requirements for eternal life in heaven?

What did it mean when Jesus likened Himself to a serpent?

Apply

What does God's love mean to you? How has He demonstrated that love?

What does it mean to you that you've been "born again"?

How can you know with confidence that you are living in the light and not the darkness?

John 3:1–21 Scripture for Memorization/Meditation

"For God so loved the world that He gave His only begotten Son, that whoever believes in Him should not perish but have everlasting life. For God did not send His Son into the world to condemn the world but that the world might be saved through Him."
VERSES 16–17

Verses for Further Memorization/Meditation

- For there is one God and one mediator between God and men, the man Christ Jesus, who gave Himself as a ransom for all (1 Timothy 2:5–6).
- To us there is but one God, the Father, from whom are all things, and we in Him, and one Lord Jesus Christ, by whom are all things, and we through Him (1 Corinthians 8:6).
- Then he called for a light and sprang in, and came trembling and fell down before Paul and Silas, and brought them out and said, "Sirs, what must I do to be saved?" And they said, "Believe in the Lord Jesus Christ, and you shall be saved, and your house" (Acts 16:29–31).

Study 22

JOHN 14:1–14

Jesus' disciples had a very real reason to feel troubled in their hearts. Jesus had just said one of them would betray Him that very night and the rest of them would deny Him at His most dire hour of need. Yet Jesus told them, "Do not let your hearts be troubled; you believe in God, believe also in Me."

Those comforting words apply to us today.

Jesus further calmed the disciples with the promise that they would one day be reunited with Him for all eternity in their home in heaven. And He stated with wonderful clarity that He alone is "the way, the truth, and the life" and the only path to God the Father.

John 14:1–14 Study Outline

(VERSES 1–4)	Jesus' words of comfort to His disciples
(VERSES 5–6)	Jesus' "I am" statement
(VERSES 7–11)	Showing the disciples the Father
(VERSES 12–14)	Precious promises

Calming the Disciples' Troubled Hearts

1 “Do not let your hearts be troubled; you believe in God, believe
also in Me. 2 In My Father’s house are many mansions; if it were
not so, I would have told you. I go to prepare a place for you.
3 And if I go and prepare a place for you, I will come again and
receive you to Myself, that where I am, there you may be also.
4 And you know where I go, and you know the way.”
5 Thomas said to Him, “Lord, we do not know where You
go, and how can we know the way?”
6 Jesus said to him, “I am the way, the truth, and the life.
No man comes to the Father except through Me.
7 “If you had known Me, you would have known My Father
also. And from now on you know Him and have seen Him.”
8 Philip said to Him, “Lord, show us the Father, and it is
sufficient for us.”
9 Jesus said to him, “Have I been with you so long, and still
you have not known Me, Philip? He who has seen Me has seen
the Father. And how do you say then, ‘Show us the Father’?
10 Do you not believe that I am in the Father and the Father in
Me? The words that I speak to you I speak not of Myself, but
the Father who dwells in Me, He does the works. 11 Believe Me
that I am in the Father and the Father in Me, or else believe
Me for the very works’ sake.
12 “Truly, truly, I say to you, he who believes in Me, the
works that I do he shall do also. And greater works than these
he shall do, because I go to My Father. 13 And whatever you ask
in My name, that I will do, that the Father may be glorified in
the Son. 14 If you ask anything in My name, I will do it.”

Observe

What was Jesus' purpose in speaking the words recorded in John 14:1–14? Why would the disciples' hearts be troubled?

....

....

....

....

....

....

What commands and promises do you see in this passage?

....

....

....

....

....

....

Where does Jesus say His words and message come from?

....

....

....

....

....

....

Interpret

Why should the disciples take comfort in Jesus' words in verses 1–3?

....

....

....

....

....

What do Jesus' seven "I am" statements in the Gospel of John (6:35, 8:12, 10:7, 10:11, 11:25, 14:6, 15:1) mean?

....

....

....

....

....

....

When Jesus says, "Whatever you ask in My name, that I will do, that the Father may be glorified in the Son," what does He really mean?

....

....

....

....

....

....

Apply

When facing difficult times, how do Jesus' promises of an eternal home with Him encourage you?

What do you think heaven will be like? What will we be doing there?

How can John 14:13–14 help to shape your daily prayer life?

John 14:1–14 Scripture for Memorization/Meditation

"Do you not believe that I am in the Father and the Father in Me? The words that I speak to you I speak not of Myself, but the Father who dwells in Me, He does the works."
VERSE 10

Verses for Further Memorization/Meditation

- For we say this to you by the word of the Lord, that we who are alive and remain until the coming of the Lord will not precede those who are asleep. For the Lord Himself shall descend from heaven with a shout, with the voice of the archangel, and with the trumpet of God. And the dead in Christ shall rise first (1 Thessalonians 4:15–16).
- Then Jesus answered and said to them, "Truly, truly, I say to you, the Son can do nothing of Himself, but what He sees the Father do. For whatever things He does, the Son likewise also does" (John 5:19).
- Then said Jesus to them, "When you have lifted up the Son of Man, then you shall know that I am He, and that I do nothing of Myself. But as My Father has taught Me, I speak these things" (John 8:28).
- I can do all things through Christ who strengthens me (Philippians 4:13).

Study 23

LUKE 1:26–38

Six months before visiting a young virgin girl named Mary, the angel Gabriel had visited a man named Zechariah in the temple in Jerusalem to announce that his older, barren wife, Elizabeth, would have a very special baby named John (see Luke 1:1–25). Now, Gabriel appeared to Mary to announce that the long-awaited Messiah would be arriving soon and that she would be His mother.

Mary's response to Gabriel's announcement was a mixture of humility, wonderment, and honest skepticism. *How can this be*, she wondered, *when I've never been with a man?* But Gabriel assured her that nothing was impossible with God and that He would keep His promise to her. Mary would give birth to Jesus Christ, God's Son and the Savior of the world.

Luke 1:26–38 Study Outline

(VERSES 26–27)	The angel Gabriel visits Mary
(VERSES 28–33)	The announcement of Jesus' birth
(VERSES 34–37)	A miracle conception
(VERSE 38)	Mary's acknowledgment

THE BIRTH OF JESUS FORETOLD

26And in the sixth month the angel Gabriel was sent from God
to a city of Galilee named Nazareth, 27to a virgin betrothed to
a man whose name was Joseph, of the house of David. And
the virgin's name was Mary. 28And the angel came in and said
to her, "Rejoice, you who are highly favored. The Lord is with
you. You are blessed among women."

29And when she saw him, she was troubled at his saying
and considered what manner of greeting this should be. 30And
the angel said to her, "Do not fear, Mary, for you have found
favor with God. 31And, behold, you shall conceive in your
womb and bring forth a Son, and shall call His name JESUS.
32He shall be great and shall be called the Son of the Highest.
And the Lord God shall give to Him the throne of His father
David. 33And He shall reign over the house of Jacob forever,
and of His kingdom there shall be no end."

34Then Mary said to the angel, "How shall this be, since I
do not know a man?"

35And the angel answered and said to her, "The Holy Spirit
shall come on you, and the power of the Highest shall over-
shadow you. Therefore, also, the Holy One who shall be born
of you shall be called the Son of God. 36And behold, your
cousin Elizabeth, she has also conceived a son in her old age,
and this is the sixth month with her who was called barren.
37For with God nothing shall be impossible."

38And Mary said, "Behold the handmaid of the Lord.
May it be to me according to your word." And the angel
departed from her.

LUKE 1:26–38

Observe

What do we learn about Gabriel in this passage? What message did he share with Mary?

....

....

....

....

....

What was her response when Gabriel informed her that she would be the mother of Jesus?

....

....

....

....

....

....

What various names and descriptions of Jesus are provided in this passage?

....

....

....

....

....

....

LUKE 1:26–38

Interpret

Why, according to Mary's visitor, was she to be the mother of the Savior?

What was the nature of Mary's question in verse 34? Was it doubt or an honest "how" inquiry? Why do you say so?

Why was it necessary for Jesus to be born of a virgin?

Apply

In what ways is Mary a role model of faith and obedience for you? How can you be more like her?

How does knowing that "with God nothing shall be impossible" help you navigate the ups and downs of life?

How might God's choice of an unknown Jewish girl to fulfill His plans encourage you today?

Luke 1:26–38 Scripture for Memorization/Meditation

And the angel said to her, "Do not fear, Mary, for you have found favor with God. And, behold, you shall conceive in your womb and bring forth a Son, and shall call His name Jesus. He shall be great and shall be called the Son of the Highest. And the Lord God shall give to Him the throne of His father David."
VERSES 30–32

"For with God nothing shall be impossible."
VERSE 37

Verses for Further Memorization/Meditation

- "Therefore the Lord Himself shall give you a sign. Behold, a virgin shall conceive and bear a son and shall call His name Immanuel" (Isaiah 7:14).
- For a Child is born to us, a Son is given to us, and the government shall be on His shoulder. And His name shall be called Wonderful, Counselor, the Mighty God, the Everlasting Father, the Prince of Peace (Isaiah 9:6).
- When the fullness of the time had come, God sent forth His Son, made of a woman, made under the law, to redeem those who were under the law, that we might receive the adoption of sons (Galatians 4:4–5).

Study 24

JOHN 1:15–34

John the Baptist was a humble man of faith who understood his God-ordained role in completing the work of bringing salvation to the world through Jesus Christ. Though John was born before Jesus, he also knew that Jesus existed before him and was infinitely greater in every way. John truly knew who Jesus was!

When the Jewish authorities sent a group of priests and Levites to question John about his identity, he was clear that he himself was not the Messiah. His role, John told his visitors, was to point others toward Jesus and to prepare them for His arrival.

John 1:15–34 Study Outline

(VERSES 15–18) John the Baptist's announcement

(VERSES 19–23) Who was John the Baptist?

(VERSES 24–28) John's baptism

(VERSES 29–34) John introduces Jesus

THE WITNESS OF JOHN THE BAPTIST

[15]John bore witness of Him and cried, saying, "This was He of whom I spoke, 'He who comes after me is preferred before me, for He was before me.'"

[16]And we have all received of His fullness, and grace for grace. [17]For the law was given by Moses, but grace and truth came by Jesus Christ. [18]No man has seen God at any time. The only begotten Son, who is in the bosom of the Father, He has declared Him.

[19]And this is the record of John, when the Jews sent priests and Levites from Jerusalem to ask him, "Who are you?" [20]And he confessed, and did not deny, but confessed, "I am not the Christ." [21]And they asked him, "What then? Are you Elijah?" And he said, "I am not." "Are you the Prophet?" And he answered, "No." [22]Then they said to him, "Who are you, that we may give an answer to those who sent us? What do you say about yourself?"

[23]He said, "I am 'the voice of one crying in the wilderness: "Make straight the way of the Lord,"' as the prophet Isaiah said."

[24]And those who were sent were of the Pharisees. [25]And they asked him and said to him, "Why then do you baptize, if you are not the Christ, nor Elijah, nor the Prophet?"

[26]John answered them, saying, "I baptize with water, but there stands One among you, whom you do not know. [27]It is He who, coming after me, is preferred before me, whose shoe strap I am not worthy to untie." [28]These things were done in Bethany beyond the Jordan, where John was baptizing.

[29]The next day John saw Jesus coming to him and said, "Behold, the Lamb of God who takes away the sin of the world. [30]This is He of whom I said, 'After me comes a Man who is preferred before me, for He was before me.' [31]And I did not know Him, but I came baptizing with water so that He would be revealed to Israel."

[32]And John bore witness, saying, "I saw the Spirit descending from heaven like a dove, and it remained on Him. [33]And I did not know Him, but He who sent me to baptize with water, the same said to me, 'On whom you shall see the Spirit descending, and remaining on Him, He is the same who baptizes with the Holy Spirit.' [34]And I saw and bore witness that this is the Son of God."

Observe

Who is John and what did he say about his mission?

....

....

....

Who did he tell the priests and Levites he *wasn't*—and who he really was?

....

....

....

....

How did John respond when he saw Jesus approaching?

....

....

....

....

Interpret

What does “the law was given by Moses, but grace and truth came by Jesus Christ” mean?

What did John, referring to Jesus as one “whose shoe strap I am not worthy to untie,” say about himself—and about Jesus?

What did it mean when John called Jesus “the Lamb of God who takes away the sin of the world”?

Apply

How can you emulate John's character qualities in your own life?

....

....

....

....

....

John was born to serve God by pointing people to Jesus. What are some ways you can point others to Jesus with your words and actions?

....

....

....

....

....

....

What does John's testimony tell you about your own value and worth in God's eyes?

....

....

....

....

....

....

JOHN 1:15–34 SCRIPTURE FOR MEMORIZATION/MEDITATION

No man has seen God at any time. The only begotten Son, who is in the bosom of the Father, He has declared Him.
VERSE 18

John answered them, saying, "I baptize with water, but there stands One among you, whom you do not know. It is He who, coming after me, is preferred before me, whose shoe strap I am not worthy to untie."
VERSES 26–27

VERSES FOR FURTHER MEMORIZATION/MEDITATION

- "Behold, I will send you Elijah the prophet before the coming of the great and dreadful day of the LORD. And he shall turn the heart of the fathers to the children and the heart of the children to their fathers, lest I come and strike the earth with a curse" (Malachi 4:5–6).
- "For all the Prophets and the Law prophesied until John. And if you will receive it, this is Elijah who is to come. He who has ears to hear, let him hear" (Matthew 11:13–15).
- And Simon Peter answered and said, "You are the Christ, the Son of the living God." And Jesus answered and said to him, "Blessed are you, Simon Bar-Jonah, for flesh and blood has not revealed it to you, but My Father who is in heaven" (Matthew 16:16–17).

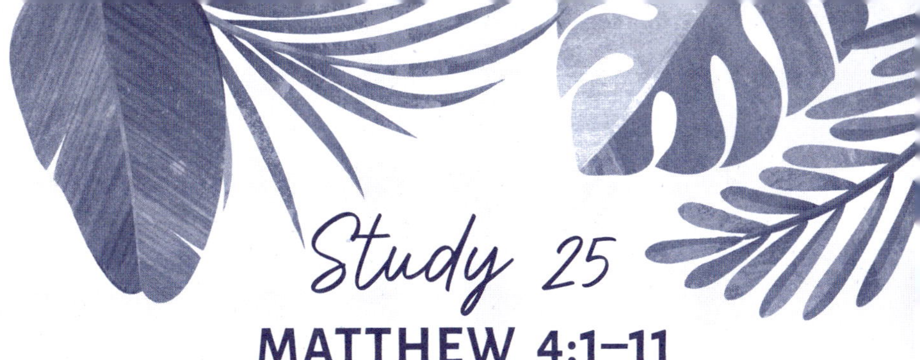

Study 25

MATTHEW 4:1–11

The writer of the book of Hebrews stated that Jesus "was in all points tempted as we are, yet without sin" (Hebrews 4:15). Yet Jesus, the Son of God and God in the flesh, was still a man, and as a man, He could be tempted to sin. After Jesus was baptized in the Jordan River, the Holy Spirit led Him into the wilderness, where the devil, trying to thwart Jesus in His mission, threw three severe temptations at Him.

When Jesus overcame those very real temptations, He kept Himself on track with the Father's plan—and also set an example for us to follow when we are tempted to sin against God.

Matthew 4:1–11 Study Outline

(VERSES 1–2)	Jesus fasts for forty days in the wilderness
(VERSES 3–4)	The devil's first temptation: turn stones to bread
(VERSES 5–7)	The devil's second temptation: leap from the top of the temple
(VERSES 8–10)	The devil's third temptation: all the world's kingdoms
(VERSE 11)	The devil leaves Jesus

Jesus Tempted in the Wilderness

[1]Then Jesus was led up by the Spirit into the wilderness to be
tempted by the devil. [2]And when He had fasted forty days and
forty nights, afterward He was hungry. [3]And when the tempter
came to Him, he said, "If You are the Son of God, command
that these stones be made bread."

[4]But He answered and said, "It is written, 'Man shall not
live by bread alone, but by every word that proceeds out of
the mouth of God.' "

[5]Then the devil took Him up into the holy city, and set
Him on a pinnacle of the temple, [6]and said to Him, "If You are
the Son of God, cast Yourself down. For it is written: 'He shall
give His angels charge concerning you,' and 'In their hands
they shall bear you up, lest at any time you dash your foot
against a stone.' "

[7]Jesus said to him, "It is written again, 'You shall not tempt
the Lord your God.' "

[8]Again, the devil took Him up on an exceedingly high
mountain and showed Him all the kingdoms of the world, and
the glory of them, [9]and said to Him, "All these things I will give
You if You will fall down and worship me."

[10]Then Jesus said to him, "Get away from here, Satan. For
it is written, 'You shall worship the Lord your God, and Him
only shall you serve.' "

[11]Then the devil left Him, and behold, angels came and
ministered to Him.

Observe

Who led Jesus into the desert? Why?

What did Jesus do during His time in the desert?

What three temptations did the devil throw at Jesus?

MATTHEW 4:1–11

Interpret

Why was the devil so intent on getting Jesus to sin?

Why would the devil first tempt Jesus to turn stones into bread?

What weapon of spiritual warfare did Jesus use to defeat the devil and send him away?

Apply

How do you usually respond when tempted by sin?

What role does God play in helping you overcome temptation?

How important are Bible reading, study, and memorization to you? What benefits have you experienced from spending time in God's Word?

Matthew 4:1–11 Scripture for Memorization/Meditation

Then Jesus said to him, "Get away from here, Satan. For it is written, 'You shall worship the Lord your God, and Him only shall you serve.'"
VERSE 10

Verses for Further Memorization/Meditation

- Your word have I hidden in my heart, that I might not sin against You (Psalm 119:11).
- For the word of God is living and powerful and sharper than any two-edged sword, piercing even to the dividing of soul and spirit, and of the joints and marrow, and is a discerner of the thoughts and intentions of the heart (Hebrews 4:12).
- And take the helmet of salvation and the sword of the Spirit, which is the word of God (Ephesians 6:17).
- All scripture is given by inspiration of God and is profitable for doctrine, for reproof, for correction, for instruction in righteousness, that the man of God may be perfect, thoroughly furnished for all good works (2 Timothy 3:16–17).

Study 26

MATTHEW 16:13–19

"Who do men say that I, the Son of Man, am?" Jesus asked His disciples—not because He wasn't perfectly aware of His own identity or because He needed human affirmation, but because He wanted His twelve closest followers to consider the true answer.

The disciples' answer to that first question showed that many didn't understand His identity or mission. But then Jesus asked the question He poses to each of us who follow Him: "Who do *you* say that I am?"

Peter heard and understood Jesus' question perfectly, and he spoke the perfect answer—and that answer would shape and guide Peter's path for the rest of his influential life on earth.

MATTHEW 16:13–19 STUDY OUTLINE

(VERSE 13)	Jesus asks His disciples who others say He is
(VERSE 14)	The disciples answer Jesus' question
(VERSE 15)	Jesus asks the disciples who *they* say He is
(VERSE 16)	Simon Peter's confession
(VERSES 17–19)	Jesus' statement of blessing

Peter's Blessed Confession

13When Jesus came into the region of Caesarea Philippi, He asked His disciples, saying, "Who do men say that I, the Son of Man, am?"

14And they said, "Some say that You are John the Baptist, some Elijah, and others Jeremiah or one of the prophets."

15He said to them, "But who do you say that I am?"

16And Simon Peter answered and said, "You are the Christ, the Son of the living God."

17And Jesus answered and said to him, "Blessed are you, Simon Bar-Jonah, for flesh and blood has not revealed it to
you, but My Father who is in heaven. 18And I also say to you
that you are Peter, and on this rock I will build My church, and
the gates of hell shall not prevail against it. 19And I will give to
you the keys of the kingdom of heaven, and whatever you bind on earth shall be bound in heaven, and whatever you loose on earth shall be loosed in heaven."

Observe

MATTHEW 16:13–19

What did the disciples' answer when Jesus asked them who others said He was?

How did Peter answer when Jesus asked the disciples who He was?

What blessing did Jesus speak to Peter after his confession?

Interpret

Why do you think Jesus first asked the disciples about who others said He was?

How was Jesus' true identity revealed to Peter? Why is that important?

What did Jesus mean when He told Peter, "I also say to you that you are Peter, and on this rock I will build My church, and the gates of hell shall not prevail against it"?

Apply

How do you answer when asked who Jesus really is?

What does it mean to you that Jesus is "the Christ, the Son of the living God"? Why is this truth important to your personal faith?

How can you be bolder in your testimony about Jesus Christ?

Matthew 16:13–19 Scripture for Memorization/Meditation

Simon Peter answered and said, "You are the Christ, the Son of the living God." And Jesus answered and said to him, "Blessed are you, Simon Bar-Jonah, for flesh and blood has not revealed it to you, but My Father who is in heaven."
VERSES 16–17

Verses for Further Memorization/Meditation

- Coming to Him, as to a living stone, rejected indeed by men, but chosen by God, and precious, you also, as living stones, are built up as a spiritual house, a holy priesthood, to offer up spiritual sacrifices acceptable to God through Jesus Christ (1 Peter 2:4–5).
- Then Peter said to them, "Repent, and every one of you be baptized in the name of Jesus Christ for the remission of sins, and you shall receive the gift of the Holy Spirit. For the promise is to you and to your children and to all who are far off, even as many as the Lord our God shall call" (Acts 2:38–39).
- Now therefore you are no longer strangers and foreigners but fellow citizens with the saints and of the household of God, and are built upon the foundation of the apostles and prophets, Jesus Christ Himself being the chief cornerstone (Ephesians 2:19–20).

Study 27

MATTHEW 26:42–56

In the moments leading up to His arrest, Jesus was alone in the garden, wrestling with the horror of what was to come. He pleaded with His Father to "let this cup pass from Me." But Jesus would accomplish the mission for which He had come to earth. This truly was the only way for Jesus to secure the salvation for humankind.

As Jesus finished His anguished prayer, a sword- and club-wielding mob arrived, intent on taking Jesus into custody. One of the disciples (identified elsewhere as Peter) unsheathed his sword and tried to violently defend his Master. But Jesus commanded him to put away his weapon, for what was happening was God's will and the fulfillment of Old Testament prophecy.

MATTHEW 26:42–56 STUDY OUTLINE

(VERSE 42)	Jesus submits in prayer to His Father
(VERSES 43–44)	Jesus finds the disciples asleep and returns to prayer
(VERSES 45–46)	The time for Jesus' arrest arrives
(VERSES 47–50)	Judas leads a mob to arrest Jesus
(VERSE 51)	Peter draws his sword and wounds one of the high priest's servants
(VERSE 52–54)	Jesus chides Peter and declares that His arrest is part of God's plan
(VERSES 55–56)	Jesus tells the mob that they are fulfilling prophecy; the disciples all flee

Jesus' Surrender in the Garden

42He went away again the second time and prayed, saying, "O My Father, if this cup may not pass away from Me unless I drink it, Your will be done." 43And He came and found them asleep again, for their eyes were heavy.

44And He left them and went away again, and prayed the third time, saying the same words. 45Then He came to His disciples and said to them, "Sleep on now, and take your rest. Behold, the hour is at hand, and the Son of Man is being betrayed into the hands of sinners. 46Rise, let us be going. Behold, he who betrays Me is at hand."

47And while He yet spoke, behold, Judas, one of the twelve, came, and with him a great multitude with swords and clubs, from the chief priests and elders of the people. 48Now he who betrayed Him gave them a sign, saying, "Whomever I kiss, that same is He. Hold Him fast." 49And immediately he came to Jesus and said, "Hail, Master," and kissed Him.

50And Jesus said to him, "Friend, why have you come?"

Then they came and laid hands on Jesus and took Him. 51And behold, one of those who was with Jesus stretched out his hand, and drew his sword, and struck a servant of the high priest, and cut off his ear.

52Then said Jesus to him, "Put up your sword into its place again, for all those who take the sword shall perish with the sword. 53Do you think that I cannot now pray to My Father, and He shall presently give Me more than twelve legions of angels? 54But how then shall the scriptures be fulfilled, that it must happen this way?"

55In that same hour Jesus said to the multitudes, "Have you come out, as against a thief, with swords and clubs to take Me? Daily I sat with you teaching in the temple, and you took no hold of Me. 56But all this was done that the scriptures of the prophets might be fulfilled."

Then all the disciples forsook Him and fled.

Observe

What did Jesus pray three times prior to His arrest in the garden of Gethsemane (verses 36–44)?

Who led the mob that came to arrest Jesus? How did he identify Jesus?

What did Peter do in an effort to defend Jesus—and how did Jesus respond?

MATTHEW 26:42–56

Interpret

What was Jesus' attitude toward the Father when He prayed, "Your will be done"?

What did Jesus reveal about Himself when He rebuked Peter for resorting to violence?

Jesus stated that He was not powerless against the crowd that came to arrest Him. Why, then, would He submit to being arrested?

Apply

MATTHEW 26:42–56

What can you do to better surrender your will to God's, even when it means suffering for Christ's sake?

What do you think when you consider that Jesus, though He understood the suffering He was about to endure, willingly gave Himself up for others?

What does Jesus' sacrifice motivate you to do for Him?

Matthew 26:42–56 Scripture for Memorization/Meditation

In that same hour Jesus said to the multitudes, "Have you come out, as against a thief, with swords and clubs to take Me? Daily I sat with you teaching in the temple, and you took no hold of Me. But all this was done that the scriptures of the prophets might be fulfilled."
VERSES 55–56

Verses for Further Memorization/Meditation

- And Jesus, going up to Jerusalem, took the twelve disciples by themselves on the road and said to them, "Behold, we are going up to Jerusalem, and the Son of Man shall be betrayed to the chief priests and to the scribes. And they shall condemn Him to death and shall deliver Him to the Gentiles to mock and to scourge and to crucify Him. And the third day He shall rise again" (Matthew 20:17–19).
- And He went a little farther and fell on His face, and prayed, saying, "O My Father, if it is possible, let this cup pass from Me. Nevertheless, not as I will, but as You will" (Matthew 26:39).
- "Therefore My Father loves Me, because I lay down My life that I might take it again. No man takes it from Me, but I lay it down of Myself. I have power to lay it down, and I have power to take it again. This commandment I have received from My Father" (John 10:17–18).

Study 28

JOHN 13:1–19

Jesus had lived His entire life in anticipation of the hour when He would give Himself up, dying a sacrificial death on a wooden cross. Until then, He had enjoyed His Father's protection from the religious authorities in Jerusalem because it was not yet time for Jesus to become the ultimate sacrifice for the sins of humankind.

Now, with His God-ordained appointment with the cross just hours away, Jesus called His disciples together to join Him for one final meal. As they finished eating, Jesus arose and did something that must have come as quite a shock to His closest followers: He washed their feet.

Peter, always one to speak his mind, strenuously objected. But Jesus had His reasons for performing such a menial task, which He lovingly explained to the disciples.

John 13:1–19 Study Outline

(VERSES 1–2)	Jesus gathers His disciples for their last Passover together
(VERSES 3–5)	Jesus begins washing the disciples' feet
(VERSES 6–8)	Jesus begins to wash Peter's feet, but Peter objects
(VERSE 9)	Peter consents
(VERSES 10–11)	Jesus knows who will betray Him
(VERSES 12–17)	Jesus explains the meaning of washing the disciples' feet
(VERSES 18–19)	Jesus foretells Judas' betrayal

The Last Passover

1Now before the Feast of the Passover, when Jesus knew that
His hour had come that He should depart out of this world to
the Father, having loved His own who were in the world, He
loved them to the end. 2And supper being ended, the devil
having now put into the heart of Judas Iscariot, Simon's son,
to betray Him, 3Jesus, knowing that the Father had given all
things into His hands, and that He had come from God and
went to God, 4He rose from supper and laid aside His garments
and took a towel and girded Himself. 5After that, He poured
water into a basin and began to wash the disciples' feet, and
to wipe them with the towel with which He was girded.

6Then He came to Simon Peter. And Peter said to Him,
"Lord, do You wash my feet?"

7Jesus answered and said to him, "What I do you do not
understand now, but you shall understand hereafter."

8Peter said to Him, "You shall never wash my feet."

Jesus answered him, "If I do not wash you, you have no
part with Me."

9Simon Peter said to Him, "Lord, not only my feet, but also
my hands and my head."

10Jesus said to him, "He who is washed needs only to wash
his feet, but is every bit clean. And you are clean, but not all."
11For He knew who would betray Him; therefore He said, "You
are not all clean." 12So after He had washed their feet, and
had taken His garments, and had sat down again, He said to
them, "Do you know what I have done to you? 13You call Me
Master and Lord, and you are right to say it, for so I am. 14If I
then, your Lord and Master, have washed your feet, you also
ought to wash one another's feet. 15For I have given you an
example, that you should do as I have done to you. 16Truly,
truly, I say to you, the servant is not greater than his master,
nor is he who is sent greater than he who sent him. 17If you

understand these things, you are happy if you do them.

[18]"I do not speak of you all. I know whom I have chosen. But that the scripture may be fulfilled, 'He who eats bread with Me has lifted up his heel against Me.' [19]Now I tell you before it comes, that when it has come to pass, you may believe that I am He."

Observe

What, according to verse 1, motivated Jesus to so humbly serve His disciples?

....

....

....

What exactly did Jesus do for the disciples after He got up from His meal?

....

....

....

....

How did Jesus answer Peter's refusal? How did Peter respond?

....

....

....

....

Interpret

Jesus washed the feet of all twelve of His disciples, including Judas. Why would He wash the feet of the man who would betray Him?

....

....

....

....

....

Why was it important for Jesus to wash His disciples' feet? What did He tell the men it meant?

....

....

....

....

....

....

What did Jesus indicate that His disciples should do in response?

....

....

....

....

....

....

Apply

Do you find it difficult to allow another person to serve you? Do you find it difficult to serve others? How does this passage speak to your attitudes?

Do you have difficulty thinking of yourself as a servant? Why or why not?

Who is someone you can serve today? How can you be a blessing to them?

John 13:1–19 Scripture for Memorization/Meditation

"I have given you an example, that you should do as I have done to you. Truly, truly, I say to you, the servant is not greater than his master, nor is he who is sent greater than he who sent him."
VERSES 15–16

Verses for Further Memorization/Meditation

- "For even the Son of Man did not come to be ministered to, but to minister, and to give His life as a ransom for many" (Mark 10:45).
- "Behold, My Servant whom I uphold, My elect in whom My soul delights. I have put My Spirit upon Him. He shall bring forth judgment to the Gentiles" (Isaiah 42:1).
- And being found in appearance as a man, He humbled Himself and became obedient to death, even the death of the cross (Philippians 2:8).
- But you were washed, but you were sanctified, but you were justified in the name of the Lord Jesus and by the Spirit of our God (1 Corinthians 6:11).

Study 29

MATTHEW 16:21–28

From the time Jesus began His ministry, He was focused on His earthly destiny: death on a Roman cross. But Jesus knew death wouldn't mean the end for Him—He would be raised from the dead and return to His Father in heaven.

Before that happened, Jesus would lovingly take time to let His disciples know what would be happening and why: it was the will of the Father and the way through which humans could be saved.

Matthew 16:21–28 Study Outline

(VERSE 21)	Jesus shows His disciples that He will die, then be raised to life again
(VERSE 22)	Peter scolds Jesus for saying He would die
(VERSE 23)	Jesus forcefully corrects Peter
(VERSES 24–28)	Jesus teaches the disciples self-denial and future rewards

Christ Foretells His Death and Resurrection

[21]From that time forth Jesus began to show to His disciples that He must go to Jerusalem, and suffer many things from the elders and chief priests and scribes, and be killed, and be raised again the third day.

[22]Then Peter took Him and began to rebuke Him, saying, "Far be it from You, Lord. This shall not happen to You."

[23]But He turned and said to Peter, "Get behind Me, Satan. You are a stumbling block to Me, for you appreciate the things that are of men, but not those that are of God."

[24]Then Jesus said to His disciples, "If any man wants to come after Me, let him deny himself, and take up his cross, and follow Me. [25]For whoever will save his life shall lose it, and whoever will lose his life for My sake shall find it. [26]For what will it profit a man if he gains the whole world and loses his own soul? Or what shall a man give in exchange for his soul? [27]For the Son of Man shall come in the glory of His Father with His angels, and then He shall reward every man according to his works. [28]Truly I say to you, there are some standing here who shall not taste of death until they see the Son of Man coming in His kingdom."

Observe

What events was Jesus preparing His disciples for?

How did Peter respond to Jesus' announcement of His own suffering and death?

What lessons did Jesus speak to the disciples after He rebuked Peter?

MATTHEW 16:21–28

Interpret

What do you learn about Peter from verse 22? What would motivate Peter to take Jesus aside and rebuke Him?

Why did Jesus respond so strongly to Peter's rebuke? What does this response tell us about Jesus?

How are Jesus' words to the disciples in verses 24–28 related to His interaction with Peter?

Apply

How would you feel if you were in the disciples' place when Jesus announced that He had to suffer and die?

When have you doubted God's plan and moved forward in your own understanding instead of following His leading? How did that turn out?

What should denying yourself and taking up your own cross look like in everyday life?

Matthew 16:21–28 Scripture for Memorization/Meditation

Jesus said to His disciples, "If any man wants to come after Me, let him deny himself, and take up his cross, and follow Me. For whoever will save his life shall lose it, and whoever will lose his life for My sake shall find it. For what will it profit a man if he gains the whole world and loses his own soul? Or what shall a man give in exchange for his soul?"
VERSES 24–26

Verses for Further Memorization/Meditation

- For we are His workmanship, created in Christ Jesus for good works, which God has before ordained that we should walk in them (Ephesians 2:10).
- As you have therefore received Christ Jesus the Lord, so walk in Him, rooted and built up in Him, and established in the faith, as you have been taught, abounding in it with thanksgiving (Colossians 2:6–7).
- And those who are Christ's have crucified the flesh with the affections and lusts. If we live in the Spirit, let us also walk in the Spirit (Galatians 5:24–25).
- Therefore be followers of God as dear children, and walk in love, as Christ has also loved us and has given Himself for us, an offering and a sacrifice to God for a sweet-smelling savor (Ephesians 5:1–2).

Study 30

MARK 9:14–29

Jesus—along with His disciples Peter, James, and John—had just descended from the Mount of Transfiguration when He saw that an argument had broken out over the other disciples' inability to heal a demon-possessed boy.

After chiding His followers for their lack of faith, Jesus met with the boy's desperate father, who knew Jesus was his son's only hope for healing. Jesus healed the boy, teaching the father about faith along the way. The Lord then took time to teach His disciples about effective faith and prayer.

Mark 9:14–29 Study Outline

(VERSES 14–16)	Jesus finds that an argument has broken out
(VERSES 17–18)	A desperate father tells Jesus about his problem
(VERSE 19)	Jesus scolds His followers for their lack of faith
(VERSES 20–21)	Jesus meets the demon-possessed boy
(VERSE 22)	The father makes his request
(VERSE 23)	Jesus encourages the man to believe
(VERSE 24)	The father's confession
(VERSES 25–27)	Jesus heals the boy
(VERSES 28–29)	Jesus teaches the disciples about prayer and fasting

The Powerless Disciples and the Mighty Christ

14And when He came to His disciples, He saw a great multitude around them, and the scribes arguing with them. 15And
immediately all the people, when they saw Him, were greatly
amazed and, running to Him, greeted Him. 16And He asked the
scribes, "What are you arguing about with them?"

17And one from the multitude answered and said, "Master, I
brought to You my son, who has a mute spirit. 18And wherever
it takes him, it tears him and he foams and gnashes with his
teeth and wastes away. And I spoke to Your disciples, that
they should cast it out, and they could not."

19He answered him and said, "O faithless generation, how
long shall I be with you? How long shall I put up with you?
Bring him to Me." 20And they brought him to Him. And when
he saw him, immediately the spirit tore him, and he fell on
the ground and wallowed, foaming. 21And He asked his father,
"How long has it been since this came to him?"

And he said, "From childhood. 22And oftentimes it has
cast him into the fire and into the waters to destroy him. But
if You can do anything, have compassion on us and help us."

23Jesus said to him, "If you can believe, all things are possible to him who believes."

24And immediately the father of the child cried out and
said with tears, "Lord, I believe; help my unbelief."

25When Jesus saw that the people came running together,
He rebuked the foul spirit, saying to it, "You mute and deaf
spirit, I charge you, come out of him, and do not enter into him
any longer!" 26And the spirit cried and tore him greatly, and
came out of him. And he was as one dead, to such an extent
that many said, "He is dead." 27But Jesus took him by the hand
and lifted him up, and he arose.

28And when He came into the house, His disciples asked

Him privately, "Why could we not cast it out?"
[29]And He said to them, "This kind cannot come out by anything except by prayer and fasting."

Observe

What is the source of the conflict in this story?

What was the desperate father's problem? What did he want Jesus to do for him? What did Jesus do in response?

What lesson did Jesus teach the disciples after performing a miracle healing?

Interpret

This same story appears in Matthew 17:14–21 but with different details. In verses 20–21, what did Jesus teach the disciples about faith?

What could the desperate father have meant when he said, "Lord, I believe; help my unbelief"?

When is fasting, in combination with prayer, needed?

Apply

Are you able to honestly express your doubts to God? How do you think He responds when you do?

In what area of your life do you need a greater measure of faith in God right now?

Why do you think the spiritual discipline of fasting is important? What has your experience with it been?

Mark 9:14–29 Scripture for Memorization/Meditation

Jesus said to him, "If you can believe, all things are possible to him who believes." And immediately the father of the child cried out and said with tears, "Lord, I believe; help my unbelief."
VERSES 23–24

Verses for Further Memorization/Meditation

- Now faith is the substance of things hoped for, the evidence of things not seen (Hebrews 11:1).
- But without faith it is impossible to please Him, for he who comes to God must believe that He is, and that He is a rewarder of those who diligently seek Him (Hebrews 11:6).
- Your faith should stand in the power of God, not in the wisdom of men (1 Corinthians 2:5).
- I am crucified with Christ; nevertheless, I live, yet not I, but Christ lives in me, and the life that I now live in the flesh I live by the faith in the Son of God, who loved me and gave Himself for me (Galatians 2:20).